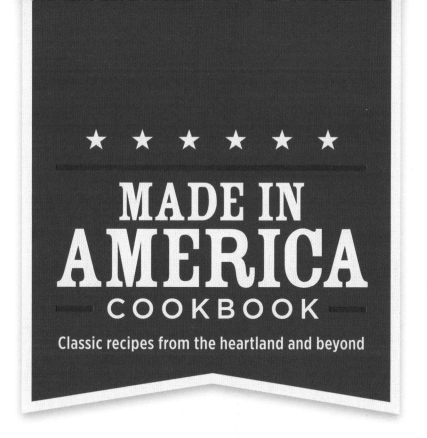

MADE IN AMERICA COOKBOOK

Classic recipes from the heartland and beyond

Publications International, Ltd.

Some of the products listed in this publication may be in limited distribution.

Front cover photography and photo on page 183 © Shutterstock.com.

Campbell's® is a registered trademark of CSC Brands LP. All rights reserved.

Pictured on the front cover: Best-Ever Apple Pie *(page 182).*

Pictured on the back cover *(top to bottom):* Strawberry Banana French Toast *(page 12),* Loaded Baked Potatoes *(page 144)* and Simple Roasted Chicken *(page 118).*

ISBN: 978-1-64558-969-3

Manufactured in China.

8 7 6 5 4 3 2 1

Microwave Cooking: Microwave ovens vary in wattage. Use the cooking times as guidelines and check for doneness before adding more time.

Let's get social!
@Publications_International
@PublicationsInternational
www.pilbooks.com

CONTENTS

BOUNTIFUL BREAKFASTS

Denver Quiche

MAKES 6 SERVINGS

★ ★

1 package (3 ounces) chicken-flavored ramen noodles*

1 tablespoon vegetable oil

½ cup diced red or green bell pepper

¼ cup diced yellow onion

½ cup diced ham

6 eggs

1 cup milk

½ cup (2 ounces) shredded Cheddar cheese

Salt and black pepper

Discard seasoning packet.

1 Preheat oven to 375°F. Spray 9-inch pie plate with nonstick cooking spray.

2 Cook noodles according to package directions. Rinse and drain under cool running water. Press noodles onto bottom of pie plate; bake 10 minutes or until lightly browned. Cool completely.

3 Heat oil in medium skillet. Add bell pepper and onion; cook 3 minutes or until crisp-tender. Add ham; cook until heated through. Spoon into crust.

4 Beat eggs and milk in medium bowl until blended. Add cheese, salt and black pepper; mix well. Carefully pour over ham mixture.

5 Bake 35 minutes or until center is puffed and knife inserted near center comes out clean. Let stand 5 minutes. Cut into wedges.

Boston Cream Bites

MAKES ABOUT 36 DOUGHNUTS

FILLING

- ½ cup granulated sugar
- 3 egg yolks
- 2 tablespoons cornstarch
- ¼ teaspoon salt
- 1 cup whole milk
- 1 tablespoon butter
- 1½ teaspoons vanilla
- Brioche Dough (recipe follows)
- Vegetable oil for frying

CHOCOLATE GLAZE

- ½ cup plus 2 tablespoons half-and-half, divided
- 1 cup semisweet or dark chocolate chips
- 1 tablespoon butter
- ½ cup powdered sugar

1 For filling, combine ½ cup granulated sugar and egg yolks in large bowl; whisk with electric mixer at medium speed about 1 minute or until pale and thickened. Whisk in cornstarch and salt. Bring milk to a simmer in medium saucepan; gradually whisk ½ cup into egg mixture. Whisk mixture into saucepan. Cook over medium-low heat about 2 minutes or until very thick, whisking constantly. Remove from heat; whisk in 1 tablespoon butter and vanilla. Press mixture through fine-mesh sieve into small bowl. Press plastic wrap directly onto surface of filling; refrigerate 1 hour or until cold.

2 Prepare Brioche Dough. Line large wire rack with paper towels.

3 Pour about 2 inches of oil into Dutch oven or large heavy saucepan; clip deep-fry or candy thermometer to side of pot. Heat over medium-high heat to 360° to 370°F.

4 Meanwhile, turn out dough onto lightly floured surface. Roll to ¼ inch thick. Cut out circles with 2-inch biscuit cutter. Working in batches, add doughnuts to hot oil. Cook 1½ minutes per side or until golden brown. Do not crowd the pan and adjust heat to maintain temperature during frying. Drain doughnuts on prepared wire rack.

5 Fit pastry bag with small round tip. Fill bag with filling. Insert thin knife into side of each doughnut and twist; pipe filling into hole.

6 Heat ½ cup half-and-half in small saucepan over low heat until bubbles form around edge of pan. Stir in chocolate chips and 1 tablespoon butter until melted and smooth. Whisk in powdered sugar and enough remaining half-and-half to make medium-thick pourable glaze. Cook 1 minute or until smooth and warm. Dip tops of doughnuts in glaze; place on wire rack and let stand until set.

Brioche Dough

★ ★ ★ ★ ★ ★ ★ ★ ★ ★ ★ ★ ★ ★ ★ ★ ★ ★ ★ ★

½ **cup water**

½ **cup milk**

1 **tablespoon active dry yeast**

½ **cup plus 1 teaspoon granulated sugar, divided**

½ **cup (1 stick) butter, softened**

3 **eggs**

½ **teaspoon vanilla**

3½ **cups all-purpose flour, divided**

¾ **teaspoon salt**

1 Heat water and milk in small saucepan to about 115°F. Remove to small bowl; stir in yeast and 1 teaspoon sugar. Let stand 5 minutes or until mixture is bubbly.

2 Beat butter and remaining ½ cup sugar in large bowl with electric mixer at medium speed until light and fluffy. Add eggs, one at a time, beating well after each addition. Beat in vanilla. Reduce speed to low; beat in yeast mixture, 1½ cups flour and salt. Beat at medium speed 2 minutes.

3 Replace beater with dough hook. Add remaining 2 cups flour. Beat at low speed until most flour is incorporated. Beat at medium speed 3 minutes (dough will be sticky). Cover and let rise in warm place 1½ hours or until doubled in size. Stir down dough. Cover and refrigerate 2 hours or overnight.

Scrambled Egg Pile-Ups

MAKES 1 SERVING

2 eggs

2 tablespoons milk

Salt and black pepper

¼ cup diced orange or red bell pepper

1 green onion, thinly sliced

¼ cup grape tomatoes, quartered (about 6 tomatoes)

⅓ cup (about 1½ ounces) shredded Cheddar cheese

1 to 2 tablespoons sour cream (optional)

1 Preheat waffle maker to medium; spray with nonstick cooking spray.

2 Whisk eggs and milk in small bowl; season lightly with salt and black pepper. Working quickly, pour egg mixture onto waffle maker, sprinkle with bell pepper, green onion and tomatoes. Close and cook 2 minutes or until puffed.

3 Remove "waffle" to plate; sprinkle with cheese and top with sour cream, if desired. Serve immediately.

TIP

To remove from waffle maker, place a plate over the egg and flip the egg onto the plate. Or, use the tip of a fork to gently release egg from waffle maker, then slide a wide spatula under to gently remove.

SERVING SUGGESTION

For a hearty breakfast, serve with hash brown potatoes and bacon.

Chocolate Doughnuts

MAKES 14 TO 16 DOUGHNUTS

2¼ cups all-purpose flour, plus additional for work surface

½ cup unsweetened cocoa powder

¼ cup cornstarch

1 teaspoon salt

1 teaspoon baking powder

½ teaspoon baking soda

½ teaspoon ground cinnamon

½ teaspoon ground nutmeg

1 cup granulated sugar

2 eggs

¼ cup (½ stick) butter, melted

¼ cup applesauce

1 teaspoon vanilla

½ cup buttermilk

Vegetable oil for frying

GLAZE

½ cup milk

1 cup semisweet or dark chocolate chips

½ teaspoon vanilla

1½ to 2 cups powdered sugar, sifted

Multicolored sprinkles

1 Whisk 2¼ cups flour, cocoa, cornstarch, salt, baking powder, baking soda, cinnamon and nutmeg in large bowl.

2 Beat 1 cup granulated sugar and eggs in large bowl with electric mixer on high speed 3 minutes or until pale and thick. Stir in butter, applesauce and 1 teaspoon vanilla. Add flour mixture alternately with buttermilk, mixing on low speed after each addition. Press plastic wrap directly onto surface of dough; refrigerate at least 1 hour.

3 Pour about 2 inches of oil into Dutch oven or large heavy saucepan; clip deep-fry or candy thermometer to side of pot. Heat over medium-high heat to 360° to 370°F.

4 Meanwhile, generously flour work surface. Turn out dough onto work surface and dust top with flour. Roll dough to about ¼-inch thickness; cut out doughnuts with floured doughnut cutter. Gather and reroll scraps. Line large wire rack with paper towels.

5 Working in batches, add doughnuts to hot oil. Cook 1 minute per side or until golden brown. Do not crowd the pan and adjust heat to maintain temperature during frying. Cool on wire racks.

6 For glaze, heat milk in small saucepan until bubbles form around edge of pan. Remove from heat. Add chocolate chips; let stand 1 minute to soften. Add ½ teaspoon vanilla; whisk until smooth. Whisk in enough powdered sugar to form stiff glaze. Dip tops of doughnuts in glaze; top with sprinkles. Let stand until glaze is set.

Strawberry Banana French Toast

MAKES 2 SERVINGS

1 cup sliced fresh
   strawberries
   (about 8 medium)

2 teaspoons granulated
   sugar

2 eggs

½ cup milk

3 tablespoons all-purpose
   flour

1 teaspoon vanilla

⅛ teaspoon salt

1 tablespoon butter

4 slices (1 inch thick) egg
   bread or country bread

1 banana, cut into ¼-inch
   slices

   Whipped cream and
   powdered sugar
   (optional)

   Maple syrup

1 Combine strawberries and granulated sugar in small bowl; toss to coat. Set aside while preparing French toast.

2 Whisk eggs, milk, flour, vanilla and salt in shallow bowl or pie plate until well blended. Melt ½ tablespoon butter in large skillet over medium-high heat. Working with two slices at a time, dip bread into egg mixture, turning to coat completely; let excess drip off. Add to skillet; cook 3 to 4 minutes per side or until golden brown. Repeat with remaining butter and bread slices.

3 Top each serving with strawberry mixture and banana slices. Garnish with whipped cream and powdered sugar; serve with maple syrup.

Smoked Salmon Omelet

MAKES 1 SERVING

3 eggs

2 tablespoons milk

1 tablespoon grated Parmesan cheese

Pinch white or black pepper

1 teaspoon butter

2 tablespoons finely chopped red onion, divided

1 ounce smoked salmon, cut into 1- to 2-inch pieces

2 tablespoons sour cream

1 tablespoon water

1 tablespoon capers, rinsed and drained

Finely chopped fresh parsley (optional)

1 Whisk eggs, milk, cheese and pepper in small bowl until well blended.

2 Heat butter in small (6-inch) nonstick skillet over medium-high heat. Pour egg mixture into skillet; stir briefly. Let eggs begin to set at edges, then lift edges and tilt skillet, allowing uncooked portion of egg mixture to flow underneath. Cook 1 minute or until omelet begins to set. Sprinkle 1 tablespoon onion over half of omelet; top with smoked salmon. Fold other half of omelet over filling; cook 1 minute. Slide omelet onto serving plate.

3 Whisk sour cream and water in small bowl until blended. Drizzle over omelet; top with remaining 1 tablespoon onion, capers and parsley, if desired.

Hearty Hash Brown Casserole ▶

MAKES ABOUT 16 SERVINGS

2 cups sour cream

2 cups (8 ounces) shredded Colby cheese, divided

1 can (10¾ ounces) cream of chicken soup

½ cup (1 stick) butter, melted

1 small onion, finely chopped

¾ teaspoon salt

½ teaspoon black pepper

1 package (30 ounces) frozen shredded hash brown potatoes, thawed

1 Preheat oven to 375°F. Spray 13×9-inch baking dish with nonstick cooking spray.

2 Combine sour cream, 1½ cups cheese, soup, butter, onion, salt and pepper in large bowl; mix well. Add potatoes; stir until well blended. Spread mixture in prepared baking dish. (Do not pack down.) Sprinkle with remaining ½ cup cheese.

3 Bake 45 minutes or until cheese is melted and top of casserole is beginning to brown.

Apple Pancakes

MAKES 10 TO 12 PANCAKES

2 tablespoons plus 2 teaspoons butter

1¼ cups milk

1 egg, beaten

1 cup all-purpose flour

¼ cup whole wheat flour

¼ cup finely chopped dried apple

¼ cup golden raisins

3 tablespoons sugar

1 tablespoon baking powder

1 teaspoon ground cinnamon

½ teaspoon salt

Maple syrup

1 Melt butter in large skillet or on griddle over medium heat. Pour into medium bowl, leaving thin film of butter on skillet. Add milk and egg; whisk until blended.

2 Combine all-purpose flour, whole wheat flour, apple, raisins, sugar, baking powder, cinnamon and salt in large bowl; mix well. Add milk mixture; stir just until blended. *Do not beat.*

3 Pour batter by ¼ cupfuls into skillet. Cook over medium heat 2 to 3 minutes per side or until golden brown. Serve with maple syrup.

★ ★ ★ ★ ★ ★

VARIATION

Substitute ¼ cup chopped pecans for the raisins.

16

Blueberry Fritter Doughnuts

MAKES 14 TO 16 DOUGHNUTS

- 2¾ cups all-purpose flour, plus additional for work surface
- ¼ cup cornstarch
- 1 teaspoon salt
- 1 teaspoon baking powder
- ½ teaspoon baking soda
- 1½ teaspoons ground cinnamon, divided
- ½ teaspoon ground nutmeg
- 1½ cups sugar, divided
- 2 eggs
- ¼ cup (½ stick) butter, melted
- ¼ cup applesauce
- 1 teaspoon vanilla
- ½ cup buttermilk
- Vegetable oil for frying
- 1 cup frozen blueberries

1 Whisk 2¾ cups flour, cornstarch, salt, baking powder, baking soda, ½ teaspoon cinnamon and nutmeg in large bowl.

2 Beat 1 cup sugar and eggs in large bowl with electric mixer on high speed 3 minutes or until pale and thick. Stir in butter, applesauce and vanilla. Add flour mixture alternately with buttermilk, mixing on low speed after each addition. Press plastic wrap directly onto surface of dough; refrigerate at least 1 hour.

3 Pour about 2 inches of oil into Dutch oven or large heavy saucepan; clip deep-fry or candy thermometer to side of pot. Heat over medium-high heat to 360° to 370°F.

4 Meanwhile, generously flour work surface. Add blueberries to dough; knead in gently. Turn out dough onto work surface and dust top with flour. Roll dough about ¼ inch thick; cut out doughnuts with floured doughnut cutter. Gather and reroll scraps. For topping, combine remaining ½ cup sugar and 1 teaspoon cinnamon in large bowl. Line large wire rack with paper towels.

5 Working in batches, add doughnuts to hot oil. Cook 1 minute per side or until golden brown. Do not crowd the pan and adjust heat to maintain temperature during frying. Drain doughnuts briefly on prepared wire rack, then sprinkle with cinnamon-sugar topping. Cool on wire rack.

NOTE

Because of the water content in the frozen blueberries, the doughnuts will pop and splatter in the oil. Use a mesh splatter screen and be careful.

Rich and Gooey Cinnamon Buns

MAKES 12 BUNS

DOUGH

- 1 package (¼ ounce) active dry yeast
- 1 cup warm milk (110°F)
- 2 eggs, beaten
- ½ cup granulated sugar
- ¼ cup (½ stick) butter, softened
- 1 teaspoon salt
- 4 to 4¼ cups all-purpose flour

FILLING

- 1 cup packed brown sugar
- 3 tablespoons ground cinnamon
  Pinch salt
- 6 tablespoons (¾ stick) butter, softened

ICING

- 1½ cups powdered sugar
- 3 ounces cream cheese, softened
- ¼ cup (½ stick) butter, softened
- ½ teaspoon vanilla
- ⅛ teaspoon salt

1 Dissolve yeast in warm milk in large bowl. Add eggs, granulated sugar, ¼ cup butter and 1 teaspoon salt; beat with electric mixer at medium speed until well blended. Add 4 cups flour; beat at low speed until dough begins to come together. Knead dough 5 minutes or until dough is smooth, elastic and slightly sticky. Add additional flour, 1 tablespoon at a time, if necessary to prevent sticking.

2 Shape dough into a ball. Place in large greased bowl; turn to grease top. Cover and let rise in warm place 1 hour or until doubled in size. Meanwhile, for filling, combine brown sugar, cinnamon and pinch of salt in small bowl; mix well.

3 Spray 13×9-inch baking pan with nonstick cooking spray. Roll out dough into 18×14-inch rectangle on floured surface. Spread 6 tablespoons butter evenly over dough; top with cinnamon-sugar mixture. Beginning with long side, roll up dough tightly jelly-roll style; pinch seam to seal. Cut log crosswise into 12 slices; place slices cut sides up in prepared pan. Cover and let rise in warm place 30 minutes or until almost doubled in size. Preheat oven to 350°F.

4 Bake 20 to 25 minutes or until golden brown. Meanwhile, for icing, combine powdered sugar, cream cheese, ¼ cup butter, vanilla and ⅛ teaspoon salt in medium bowl; beat with electric mixer at medium speed 2 minutes or until smooth and creamy. Spread icing generously over warm cinnamon buns.

Sweet Potato Pancakes

MAKES 5 SERVINGS (10 LARGE PANCAKES)

PANCAKES

- 2 medium sweet potatoes
- 2½ cups all-purpose flour
- 1 teaspoon baking powder
- 1 teaspoon baking soda
- ½ teaspoon salt
- ½ teaspoon ground cinnamon
- ¼ teaspoon ground ginger
- 2¾ cups buttermilk
- 2 eggs
- 2 tablespoons packed brown sugar
- 2 tablespoons butter, melted and cooled, plus additional for pan

GINGER BUTTER

- ¼ cup (½ stick) butter, softened
- 1 tablespoon packed brown sugar
- 1 teaspoon grated fresh ginger
- Pinch salt
- Prepared caramel sauce or maple syrup
- ¾ cup chopped glazed pecans*

Glazed or candied pecans may be found in the produce section of the supermarket along with other salad convenience items, or they may be found in the snack aisle.

1 Preheat oven to 375°F. Scrub sweet potatoes; bake 50 to 60 minutes or until soft. Cool slightly; peel and mash. Measure out 1⅓ cups for pancake batter.

2 Combine flour, baking powder, baking soda, salt, cinnamon and ground ginger in medium bowl; mix well. Whisk buttermilk, eggs and 2 tablespoons brown sugar in large bowl until well blended. Stir in 2 tablespoons melted butter. Add sweet potatoes; whisk until well blended. Add flour mixture; stir just until dry ingredients are moistened and no streaks of flour remain. Do not overmix; batter will be lumpy. Let stand 10 minutes.

3 Heat griddle or large skillet* over medium heat; brush with melted butter to coat. For each pancake, pour ½ cup of batter onto griddle, spreading into 5- to 6-inch circle. Cook 4 minutes or until bottom is golden brown and small bubbles appear on surface. Turn pancake; cook 3 minutes or until golden brown. Add additional butter to griddle as needed.

4 For ginger butter, beat ¼ cup softened butter, 1 tablespoon brown sugar, fresh ginger and pinch of salt in small bowl until well blended. If using caramel sauce, microwave according to package directions. Stir in water, 1 teaspoon at a time, to thin to desired pouring consistency.

5 Serve pancakes warm topped with ginger butter, caramel sauce and glazed pecans.

Stuffed Hash Browns

MAKES 1 TO 2 SERVINGS

1½ **cups shredded potatoes***

2 **tablespoons finely chopped onion**

¼ **plus ⅛ teaspoon salt, divided**

⅛ **teaspoon black pepper**

2 **tablespoons butter, divided**

1 **tablespoon vegetable oil**

½ **cup diced ham (¼-inch pieces)**

3 **eggs**

2 **tablespoons milk**

2 **slices American cheese**

*Use refrigerated shredded hash brown potatoes or shredded peeled russet potatoes, squeezed dry.

1 Preheat oven to 250°F. Place wire rack over baking sheet. Combine potatoes, onion, ¼ teaspoon salt and pepper in medium bowl; mix well.

2 Heat 1 tablespoon butter and oil in small (6- to 8-inch) nonstick skillet over medium heat. Add potato mixture; spread to cover bottom of skillet evenly, pressing down gently with spatula to flatten. Cook 10 minutes or until bottom and edges are golden brown. Cover skillet with large inverted plate; carefully flip hash browns onto plate. Slide hash browns back into skillet, cooked side up. Cook 10 minutes or until golden brown. Slide hash browns onto prepared wire rack; place in oven to keep warm while preparing ham and eggs.

3 Melt 1 teaspoon butter in same skillet over medium-high heat. Add ham; cook and stir 2 to 3 minutes or until lightly browned. Remove to plate.

4 Whisk eggs, milk and remaining ⅛ teaspoon salt in small bowl. Melt remaining 2 teaspoons butter in same skillet over medium-high heat. Add egg mixture; cook 3 minutes or just until eggs are cooked through, stirring to form large, fluffy curds. Place cheese slices on top of eggs; remove from heat and cover skillet with lid or foil to melt cheese.

5 Place hash browns on serving plate; sprinkle one side of hash browns with ham. Top ham with eggs; fold hash browns in half over eggs.

TIP

Refrigerated shredded potatoes are very wet when removed from the package. For the best results, dry them well with paper towels before cooking.

Jelly Doughnuts

MAKES 22 TO 24 DOUGHNUTS

BRIOCHE DOUGH

- ½ cup water
- ½ cup milk
- 1 tablespoon active dry yeast
- ½ cup plus 1 teaspoon granulated sugar, divided
- ½ cup (1 stick) butter, softened
- 3 eggs
- ½ teaspoon vanilla
- 3½ cups all-purpose flour, divided
- ¾ teaspoon salt
- Vegetable oil for frying

FILLING

- 1 cup seedless raspberry jam
- Powdered sugar

1 Heat water and milk in small saucepan to about 115°F. Remove to small bowl; stir in yeast and 1 teaspoon granulated sugar. Let stand 5 minutes or until mixture is bubbly.

2 Beat butter and remaining ½ cup granulated sugar in large bowl with electric mixer at medium speed until light and fluffy. Add eggs, one at a time, beating well after each addition. Beat in vanilla. Reduce speed to low; beat in yeast mixture, 1½ cups flour and salt. Beat at medium speed 2 minutes.

3 Add remaining 2 cups flour. Beat at low speed until most flour is incorporated. Beat at medium speed 3 minutes (dough will be sticky). Cover and let rise in warm place about 1½ hours or until doubled in size. Stir down dough. Cover and refrigerate 2 hours or overnight.

4 Pour about 2 inches of oil into Dutch oven or large heavy saucepan; clip deep-fry or candy thermometer to side of pot. Heat over medium-high heat to 360° to 370°F.

5 Meanwhile, turn out dough onto lightly floured surface. Roll ¼ inch thick. Cut out circles with 2-inch biscuit cutter. Line large wire rack with paper towels.

6 Working in batches, add doughnuts to hot oil. Cook 1½ minutes per side or until golden brown. Do not crowd the pan and adjust heat to maintain temperature during frying. Drain doughnuts on prepared wire rack.

7 Fit pastry bag with small round tip. Fill bag with jam. Insert thin knife into side of each doughnut and twist to make room for jam. Fill doughnuts with jam; sprinkle with powdered sugar.

APPETIZERS
AND
DRINKS

Buffalo Chicken Dip

MAKES 5 CUPS

2 packages (8 ounces each) cream cheese, softened and cut into pieces

1 jar (12 ounces) restaurant-style wing sauce

1 cup ranch dressing

2 cups shredded cooked chicken (from 1 pound boneless skinless chicken breasts)

2 cups (8 ounces) shredded Cheddar cheese

Tortilla chips

Celery sticks

1 Combine cream cheese, wing sauce and ranch dressing in large saucepan; cook over medium-low heat 7 to 10 minutes or until cream cheese is melted and mixture is smooth, whisking frequently.

2 Combine chicken and Cheddar cheese in large bowl. Add cream cheese mixture; stir until well blended. Pour into serving bowl; serve warm with tortilla chips and celery sticks.

Chicken Parmesan Sliders

MAKES 12 SLIDERS

- 4 boneless skinless chicken breasts (6 to 8 ounces each)
- ¼ cup all-purpose flour
- 2 eggs
- 1 tablespoon water
- 1 cup Italian-seasoned dry bread crumbs
- ½ cup grated Parmesan cheese
    Salt and black pepper
    Olive oil
- 12 slider buns (about 3 inches), split
- ¾ cup marinara sauce
- 6 tablespoons Alfredo sauce
- 6 slices mozzarella cheese, cut into halves
- 2 tablespoons butter, melted
- ¼ teaspoon garlic powder
- 6 tablespoons pesto

1 Preheat oven to 375°F. Line medium baking sheet with foil; top with wire rack.

2 Pound chicken to ½-inch thickness between two sheets of waxed paper or plastic wrap with meat mallet or rolling pin. Cut each chicken breast crosswise into three pieces about the size of slider buns.

3 Place flour in shallow dish. Beat eggs and water in second shallow dish. Combine bread crumbs and Parmesan in third shallow dish. Season flour and egg mixtures with pinch of salt and pepper. Coat chicken pieces lightly with flour, shaking off excess. Dip in egg mixture, coating completely; roll in bread crumb mixture to coat. Place on large plate; let stand 10 minutes.

4 Heat ¼ inch oil in large nonstick skillet over medium-high heat. Add chicken in single layer (cook in two batches if necessary); cook 3 to 4 minutes per side or until golden brown. Remove chicken to wire rack; bake 5 minutes or until cooked through (165°F). Remove rack with chicken from baking sheet.

5 Arrange slider buns on medium foil-lined baking sheet with bottoms cut sides up and tops cut sides down. Spread 1 tablespoon marinara sauce over each bottom bun; top with piece of chicken. Spread ½ tablespoon Alfredo sauce over chicken; top with half slice of mozzarella. Combine butter and garlic powder in small bowl; brush mixture over top buns.

6 Bake 3 to 4 minutes or until mozzarella is melted and top buns are lightly toasted. Spread ½ tablespoon pesto over mozzarella; cover with top buns.

Pretzel Sticks with Beer-Cheese Dip

MAKES 6 TO 8 SERVINGS (2 CUPS DIP)

★ ★

PRETZELS

- 1⅔ cups warm water (110° to 115°F)
- 1 package (¼ ounce) active dry yeast
- 2 teaspoons sugar
- 1 teaspoon table salt
- 4½ cups all-purpose flour, plus additional for work surface
- 2 tablespoons butter, softened
- 2 tablespoons vegetable oil
- 12 cups water
- ½ cup baking soda
  Kosher salt or pretzel salt and sesame seeds

HONEY-MUSTARD DIP

- ⅓ cup sour cream
- ¼ cup Dijon mustard
- 3 tablespoons honey

BEER-CHEESE DIP

- 2 tablespoons butter
- 1 clove garlic, minced
- 2 tablespoons all-purpose flour
- 1 tablespoon Dijon mustard
- 1 teaspoon Worcestershire sauce
- 1 cup Belgian white ale
- 2 cups (8 ounces) shredded white Cheddar cheese
- 1 cup (4 ounces) shredded Monterey Jack cheese
  Black pepper (optional)

1 For pretzels, combine 1⅔ cups warm water, yeast, sugar and 1 teaspoon table salt in large bowl; stir to dissolve yeast. Let stand 5 minutes or until bubbly. Add 4½ cups flour and softened butter; beat with electric mixture at low speed until combined, scraping side of bowl occasionally. Remove dough to lightly floured surface. Knead 5 minutes. Place dough in large greased bowl; turn to coat top. Cover and let rise in warm place 1 hour or until doubled in size.

2 For mustard dip, combine sour cream, ¼ cup mustard and honey in small bowl; mix well. Refrigerate until ready to use.

3 Preheat oven to 450°F. Brush 1 tablespoon oil over each of two large baking sheets. Bring 12 cups water to a boil in large saucepan or Dutch oven.

4 Punch down dough; turn out onto floured work surface. Cut dough into 14 equal pieces. Roll each piece into 12-inch-long rope. Cut each rope in half.

5 Carefully stir baking soda into boiling water. Working in batches, drop dough pieces into boiling water; cook 30 seconds. Remove to prepared baking sheets with slotted spoon. Make 3 to 4 slashes in each pretzel stick with sharp knife. Sprinkle with kosher salt and sesame seeds.

6 Bake 14 to 15 minutes or until dark golden brown, rotating baking sheets halfway through baking time. Cool slightly on wire rack.

7 Meanwhile for cheese dip, melt 2 tablespoons butter in medium saucepan over medium heat. Add garlic; cook and stir 1 minute. Whisk in 2 tablespoons flour until well blended; cook 1 minute. Whisk in 1 tablespoon mustard and

Worcestershire sauce. Slowly whisk in ale in thin steady stream. Cook 1 minute or until slightly thickened. Add cheeses by ¼ cupfuls, stirring until cheeses are melted before adding next addition. Remove to serving bowl; sprinkle with pepper, if desired. Serve pretzels warm with dips.

Buffalo Wings ▶

MAKES 4 SERVINGS

1 cup hot pepper sauce

⅓ cup vegetable oil, plus additional for frying

1 teaspoon sugar

½ teaspoon ground red pepper

½ teaspoon garlic powder

½ teaspoon Worcestershire sauce

⅛ teaspoon black pepper

1 pound chicken wings, tips discarded, separated at joints

Blue cheese or ranch dressing

Celery sticks

1 Combine hot pepper sauce, ⅓ cup oil, sugar, red pepper, garlic powder, Worcestershire sauce and black pepper in small saucepan; cook over medium heat 20 minutes. Place large wire rack over paper towels. Pour sauce into large bowl.

2 Heat 3 inches of oil in large saucepan over medium-high heat to 350°F; adjust heat to maintain temperature during frying. Add wings; cook 10 minutes or until crispy. Drain on prepared wire rack.

3 Remove wings to bowl of sauce; toss to coat. Serve with blue cheese dressing and celery sticks.

Old Fashioned

MAKES 1 SERVING

1 sugar cube

2 dashes Angostura bitters

1 teaspoon water

2 ounces whiskey

Lemon peel twist

Place sugar cube, bitters and water in old fashioned glass; muddle until sugar is dissolved. Fill glass half full with ice; stir in whiskey and lemon twist.

Mozzarella Sticks ▶

MAKES 4 TO 6 SERVINGS

¼ cup all-purpose flour

2 eggs

1 tablespoon water

1 cup plain dry bread crumbs

2 teaspoons Italian seasoning

½ teaspoon salt

½ teaspoon garlic powder

1 package (12 ounces) string cheese (12 sticks)

Vegetable oil for frying

1 cup marinara or pizza sauce, heated

1 Place flour in shallow bowl. Whisk eggs and water in another shallow bowl. Combine bread crumbs, Italian seasoning, salt and garlic powder in third shallow bowl. Place large wire rack over paper towels.

2 Coat each piece of cheese with flour. Dip in egg mixture, letting excess drip back into bowl. Roll in bread crumb mixture to coat. Dip again in egg mixture and roll again in bread crumb mixture. Place on plate; refrigerate until ready to cook.

3 Heat 2 inches of oil in large saucepan over medium-high heat to 350°F; adjust heat to maintain temperature. Add cheese sticks; cook 1 minute or until golden brown. Drain on prepared wire rack. Serve with warm marinara sauce for dipping.

Mini Dizzy Dogs

MAKES 20 APPETIZERS

½ sheet refrigerated crescent roll dough (half of 8-ounce package)

20 mini hot dogs or smoked sausages

Ketchup and mustard

1 Preheat oven to 375°F. Line baking sheet with parchment paper.

2 Cut dough lengthwise into 20 (¼-inch) strips. Coil 1 dough strip around 1 hot dog. Place on prepared baking sheet.

3 Bake 10 to 12 minutes or until light golden brown. Serve with ketchup and mustard for dipping.

Potato Skins ▶

MAKES 8 SERVINGS

- 8 medium baking potatoes (6 to 8 ounces each), unpeeled
- 1 tablespoon vegetable oil
- 1 teaspoon salt
- ⅛ teaspoon black pepper
- 1 tablespoon butter, melted
- 1 cup (4 ounces) shredded Cheddar cheese
- 8 slices bacon, crisp-cooked and coarsely chopped
- 1 cup sour cream
- 3 tablespoons snipped fresh chives

1 Preheat oven to 400°F.

2 Prick potatoes all over with fork. Rub oil over potatoes; sprinkle with salt and pepper. Place in 13×9-inch baking pan. Bake 1 hour or until fork-tender. Let stand until cool enough to handle. *Reduce oven temperature to 350°F.*

3 Cut potatoes in half lengthwise; cut small slice off bottom of each half so potato halves lay flat. Scoop out soft middles of potato skins; reserve for another use. Place potato halves, skin sides up, in baking pan; brush potato skins with butter.

4 Bake 20 to 25 minutes or until crisp. Turn potatoes over; top with cheese and bacon. Bake 5 minutes or until cheese is melted. Cool slightly. Top with sour cream and chives just before serving.

Manhattan

MAKES 1 SERVING

- 2 ounces whiskey
- 1 ounce sweet vermouth
- 1 dash Angostura bitters
  Maraschino cherry

Fill cocktail shaker half full with ice; add whiskey, vermouth and bitters. Stir until blended; strain into chilled cocktail glass or ice-filled old fashioned glass. Garnish with maraschino cherry.

Green Bean Fries

MAKES 4 TO 6 SERVINGS

DIP

- ½ cup mayonnaise
- ¼ cup sour cream
- ¼ cup buttermilk
- ¼ cup minced peeled cucumber
- 1½ teaspoons lemon juice
- 1 clove garlic
- 1 teaspoon wasabi powder
- 1 teaspoon prepared horseradish
- ½ teaspoon dried dill weed
- ½ teaspoon dried parsley flakes
- ½ teaspoon salt
- ⅛ teaspoon ground red pepper

GREEN BEAN FRIES

- 8 ounces fresh green beans, trimmed
- ½ cup all-purpose flour
- ½ cup cornstarch
- ¾ cup milk
- 1 egg
- 1 cup plain dry bread crumbs
- 1 teaspoon salt
- ½ teaspoon onion powder
- ¼ teaspoon garlic powder
- Vegetable oil for frying

1 For dip, combine mayonnaise, sour cream, buttermilk, cucumber, lemon juice, garlic, wasabi, horseradish, dill, parsley flakes, salt and red pepper in blender; blend until smooth. Refrigerate until ready to use.

2 For fries, bring large saucepan of salted water to a boil. Add green beans; cook 4 minutes or until crisp-tender. Drain and run under cold running water to stop cooking.

3 Combine flour and cornstarch in large bowl. Whisk milk and egg in another large bowl. Combine bread crumbs, salt, onion powder and garlic powder in shallow bowl. Place green beans in flour mixture; toss to coat. Working in batches, coat beans with egg mixture, letting excess drain back into bowl. Roll beans in bread crumb mixture to coat. Place on large baking sheet.

4 Heat 3 inches of oil in large saucepan over medium-high heat to 375°F. Cook green beans in batches 1 minute or until golden brown; adjust heat to maintain temperature during frying. Drain on paper towel-lined plate. Serve warm with dip.

Cheesy Garlic Bread ▶

MAKES 8 TO 10 SERVINGS

1 loaf (about 16 ounces) Italian bread

½ cup (1 stick) butter, softened

8 cloves garlic, very thinly sliced

¼ cup grated Parmesan cheese

2 cups (8 ounces) shredded mozzarella cheese

1 Preheat oven to 425°F. Line large baking sheet with foil.

2 Cut bread in half horizontally. Spread cut sides of bread evenly with butter; top with sliced garlic. Sprinkle with Parmesan cheese, then mozzarella cheese. Place on prepared baking sheet.

3 Bake 12 minutes or until cheeses are melted and golden brown in spots. Cut bread crosswise into slices. Serve warm.

Classic Deviled Eggs

MAKES 12 DEVILED EGGS

6 eggs

3 tablespoons mayonnaise

½ teaspoon apple cider vinegar

½ teaspoon yellow mustard

⅛ teaspoon salt

Optional toppings: black pepper, paprika, minced fresh chives and/or minced red onion (optional)

1 Bring medium saucepan of water to a boil. Gently add eggs with slotted spoon. Reduce heat to maintain a simmer; cook 12 minutes. Meanwhile, fill medium bowl with cold water and ice cubes. Drain eggs and place in ice water; cool 10 minutes.

2 Carefully peel eggs. Cut eggs in half; place yolks in small bowl. Add mayonnaise, vinegar, mustard and salt; mash until well blended. Spoon mixture into egg whites; garnish with desired toppings.

Fried Macaroni and Cheese Bites

MAKES 48 PIECES (ABOUT 8 SERVINGS)

8 ounces uncooked elbow macaroni

2 tablespoons butter

2 tablespoons all-purpose flour

2 cups milk

1 teaspoon salt, divided

2 cups (8 ounces) shredded Cheddar cheese

1 cup (4 ounces) shredded Swiss cheese

1 cup (4 ounces) shredded smoked Gouda cheese

Vegetable oil for frying

3 eggs

¼ cup water

2 cups plain dry bread crumbs

1 teaspoon Italian seasoning

Marinara sauce, heated

1 Cook macaroni in large saucepan of boiling salted water 7 minutes or until al dente. Drain and set aside.

2 Melt butter in same saucepan over medium-high heat. Whisk in flour until smooth. Cook 1 minute, whisking frequently. Whisk in milk in thin, steady stream; cook over medium-high heat 8 minutes or until thickened. Add ½ teaspoon salt. Gradually stir in cheeses until melted and smooth. Stir in macaroni.

3 Spray 9-inch square baking pan with nonstick cooking spray. Spread macaroni and cheese in prepared pan; smooth top. Cover with plastic wrap; refrigerate 4 hours or until firm and cold.

4 Turn out macaroni and cheese onto cutting board; cut into 48 pieces. Heat ½ inch of oil in large deep skillet or saucepan to 350°F over medium-high heat.

5 Whisk eggs and ¼ cup water in medium bowl. Combine bread crumbs, Italian seasoning and remaining ½ teaspoon salt in another medium bowl. Working with a few pieces at a time, dip macaroni and cheese pieces in egg, then toss in bread crumb mixture to coat. Place on large baking sheet. Dip coated pieces in egg mixture again; toss in bread crumb mixture to coat.

6 Fry in batches 3 minutes or until dark golden brown, turning once. Remove to paper towel-lined wire rack. Return oil to 350°F between batches. Serve warm with marinara sauce for dipping.

Onion Ring Stack

MAKES 4 TO 6 SERVINGS (ABOUT 20 ONION RINGS)

- 1 cup all-purpose flour, divided
- ½ cup cornmeal
- 1 teaspoon black pepper
- ½ teaspoon salt, plus additional for seasoning
- ¼ to ½ teaspoon ground red pepper
- 1 cup light-colored beer
  Rémoulade Sauce (recipe follows) or ranch dressing
  Vegetable oil for frying
- 6 tablespoons cornstarch, divided
- 2 large sweet onions, cut into ½-inch rings and separated

1 Combine ½ cup flour, cornmeal, black pepper, ½ teaspoon salt and red pepper in large bowl; mix well. Whisk in beer until well blended. Let batter stand 1 hour.

2 Prepare Rémoulade Sauce; refrigerate until ready to serve.

3 Pour 2 inches of oil into large saucepan or Dutch oven; heat to 360° to 370°F. Line large wire rack with paper towels.

4 Whisk 4 tablespoons cornstarch into batter. Combine remaining ½ cup flour and 2 tablespoons cornstarch in medium bowl. Thoroughly coat onions with flour mixture.

5 Working with one at a time, dip onion rings into batter to coat completely; carefully place in hot oil. Cook about 4 onion rings at a time 3 minutes or until golden brown, turning once. Remove to prepared wire rack; season with additional salt. Return oil to 370°F between batches. Serve immediately with Rémoulade Sauce.

RÉMOULADE SAUCE

Combine 1 cup mayonnaise, 2 tablespoons coarse-grain mustard, 1 tablespoon lemon juice, 1 tablespoon sweet relish, 1 teaspoon horseradish sauce, 1 teaspoon Worcestershire sauce and ¼ teaspoon hot pepper sauce in medium bowl; mix well.

Pepperoni Bread ▶

MAKES ABOUT 6 SERVINGS

★ ★

1 package (about 14 ounces) refrigerated pizza dough

8 slices provolone cheese

20 to 30 slices pepperoni (about half of 6-ounce package)

½ teaspoon Italian seasoning

¾ cup (3 ounces) shredded mozzarella cheese

½ cup grated Parmesan cheese

1 egg, beaten

Marinara sauce, heated

1 Preheat oven to 400°F. Unroll pizza dough on sheet of parchment paper with long side in front of you. Cut off corners of dough to create oval shape.

2 Arrange half of provolone cheese slices over bottom half of oval, cutting to fit as necessary. Top with pepperoni; sprinkle with ¼ teaspoon Italian seasoning. Top with mozzarella cheese, Parmesan cheese and remaining provolone cheese slices; sprinkle with remaining ¼ teaspoon Italian seasoning.

3 Fold top half of dough over filling to create half moon (calzone) shape; press edges with fork or pinch edges to seal. Transfer calzone with parchment paper to large baking sheet; curve slightly into crescent shape. Brush with beaten egg.

4 Bake 16 minutes or until crust is golden brown. Remove to wire rack to cool slightly. Cut crosswise into slices; serve warm with marinara sauce.

Americano

MAKES 1 SERVING

★ ★

1½ ounces sweet vermouth

1½ ounces Campari

Chilled club soda

Lemon wedge

Fill glass with ice. Pour vermouth and Campari over ice; fill with club soda. Garnish with lemon wedge.

Jalapeño Poppers

MAKES 20 TO 24 POPPERS

10 to 12 fresh jalapeño peppers*

1 package (8 ounces) cream cheese, softened

1½ cups (6 ounces) shredded Cheddar cheese, divided

2 green onions, finely chopped

½ teaspoon onion powder

¼ teaspoon salt

⅛ teaspoon garlic powder

6 slices bacon, crisp-cooked and finely chopped

2 tablespoons almond flour (optional)

2 tablespoons grated Parmesan or Romano cheese

For large jalapeño peppers, use 10. For small peppers, use 12.

1 Preheat oven to 375°F. Line baking sheet with parchment paper or foil.

2 Cut each jalapeño pepper in half lengthwise; remove ribs and seeds.

3 Combine cream cheese, 1 cup Cheddar cheese, green onions, onion powder, salt and garlic powder in medium bowl. Stir in bacon. Fill each jalapeño pepper half with about 1 tablespoon cheese mixture. Place on prepared baking sheet. Sprinkle with remaining ½ cup Cheddar cheese, almond flour, if desired, and Parmesan cheese.

4 Bake 10 to 12 minutes or until cheeses are melted and jalapeño peppers are slightly softened.

Beer-Battered Shrimp ▶

MAKES 4 TO 6 SERVINGS

- ¾ cup mayonnaise
- ⅓ cup Thai sweet chili-garlic sauce
- 1¼ cups all-purpose flour
- 1 teaspoon baking powder
- ½ teaspoon sweet paprika
- ½ teaspoon salt
- 1 bottle (12 ounces) lager, as needed
  Vegetable oil for frying
- 1½ pounds raw shrimp, peeled and deveined

1 Combine mayonnaise and chili-garlic sauce in medium bowl; mix well. Cover; refrigerate at least 2 hours or up to 2 days.

2 Whisk flour, baking powder, paprika and salt in medium bowl. Whisk in enough lager to make thick batter. Cover; let stand at room temperature 2 to 4 hours.

3 Preheat oven to 200°F. Fill large heavy, deep saucepan half full with oil; heat over high heat to 350°F. Line large baking sheet with paper towels.

4 Working in batches, dip shrimp in batter, letting excess drip back into bowl. Carefully add shrimp to oil; cook 2½ minutes or until golden brown. Remove to prepared baking sheet with slotted spoon. Keep warm in oven while frying remaining shrimp. Serve warm with dip.

Mint Julep

MAKES 1 SERVING

- 4 to 6 fresh mint leaves
- 1 teaspoon sugar
- 3 ounces bourbon
  Sprig fresh mint

Muddle mint leaves and sugar in glass. Fill glass with ice; pour in bourbon. Garnish with mint sprig.

Chili Cheese Fries ▶

MAKES 4 SERVINGS

★ ★ ★ ★ ★ ★ ★ ★ ★ ★ ★ ★ ★ ★ ★ ★ ★ ★ ★ ★

1½ pounds ground beef

1 medium onion, chopped

2 cloves garlic, minced

½ cup lager

2 tablespoons chili powder

2 tablespoons tomato paste

Salt and black pepper

1 package (32 ounces) frozen French fries

1 jar (15 ounces) cheese sauce, heated

Sour cream and chopped green onions (optional)

1 Brown beef, onion and garlic in large skillet over medium-high heat 6 to 8 minutes, stirring to break up meat. Drain fat.

2 Stir lager, chili powder and tomato paste into beef mixture. Simmer, stirring occasionally, 20 minutes or until most liquid has evaporated. Season with salt and pepper.

3 Meanwhile, bake French fries according to package directions.

4 Divide French fries evenly among bowls. Top evenly with chili and cheese sauce. Garnish with sour cream and green onions.

Sazerac

MAKES 1 SERVING

2 ounces whiskey

¼ ounce anise-flavored liqueur

½ ounce simple syrup*

Dash of bitters

To make simple syrup, bring 1 cup water to a boil; stir in 1 cup sugar. Reduce heat to low; stir constantly until sugar is dissolved. Cool syrup to room temperature; store in glass jar in refrigerator.

Fill cocktail shaker half full with ice; add whiskey, liqueur, syrup and bitters. Stir until blended; strain into old fashioned glass.

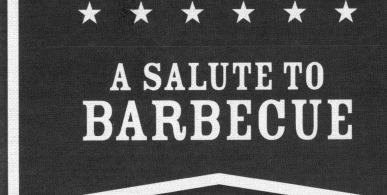

All-American Barbecue Grilled Chicken

MAKES 6 SERVINGS

★ ★

1 sheet REYNOLDS WRAP® Non-Stick Foil
6 chicken pieces
1 cup southwestern barbecue sauce

HEAT grill to medium-high. Make drainage holes in sheet of REYNOLDS WRAP® Non-Stick Foil with a large fork. Place foil sheet on grill grate with non-stick (dull) side facing up; immediately place chicken on foil.

GRILL covered 10 minutes. Turn chicken; brush chicken with barbecue sauce. Grill 10 minutes longer; turn chicken. Brush again with barbecue sauce; continue grilling until chicken is tender and reaches 180°F. Discard any remaining sauce.

★ ★ ★ ★ ★ ★

SOUTHWESTERN BARBECUE SAUCE

Add 2 teaspoons chili powder, 1 teaspoon dry mustard, ¼ teaspoon garlic powder and ¼ teaspoon cayenne pepper to barbecue sauce. Grill as directed above.

Beer-Basted Barbecue Pork Chops

MAKES 6 SERVINGS

1 cup prepared barbecue
   sauce, divided
1 cup plus 3 tablespoons
   beer, divided
3 tablespoons honey
1 tablespoon chili powder
6 bone-in loin pork chops,
   cut about 1 inch thick
1 teaspoon salt
½ teaspoon black pepper

1 Combine ½ cup barbecue sauce, 1 cup beer, honey and chili powder in large bowl. Add pork chops, turning to coat; refrigerate 2 to 4 hours, turning occasionally. Combine remaining ½ cup barbecue sauce and 3 tablespoons beer in separate bowl; set aside.

2 Prepare grill for direct cooking over medium-high heat. Oil grid.

3 Remove pork chops from beer mixture and sprinkle with salt and pepper. Place pork chops on prepared grid over medium-high heat. Grill 4 minutes. Turn chops over; brush with half of reserved barbecue sauce mixture. Grill 3 minutes. Turn over; brush with remaining sauce mixture and grill 4 to 5 minutes or until an instant read thermometer inserted into the thickest portion of pork chops registers 150°F.

Western Barbecue Burgers with Beer Barbecue Sauce ▶

MAKES 4 SERVINGS

1½ pounds ground beef

1 cup smokehouse-style barbecue sauce

¼ cup brown ale

½ teaspoon salt

¼ teaspoon black pepper

1 red onion, cut into ½-inch-thick slices

4 hamburger buns

8 slices thick-cut bacon, crisp-cooked

Tomato slices

Lettuce leaves

1 Prepare grill for direct cooking over medium-high heat. Shape beef into four patties, about ¾ inch thick.

2 Combine barbecue sauce, ale, salt and pepper in small saucepan. Bring to a boil; boil 1 minute. Set aside.

3 Grill burgers, covered, 8 to 10 minutes or to desired doneness, turning occasionally. Grill onion 4 minutes or until softened and slightly charred, turning occasionally.

4 Serve burgers on buns with onion, bacon, barbecue sauce mixture, tomatoes and lettuce.

Kansas City Barbecue Sauce

MAKES 2 CUPS

1½ cups ketchup

⅓ cup packed light brown sugar

¼ cup molasses

¼ cup cider vinegar

1 tablespoon dry mustard

2 teaspoons onion powder

2 teaspoons chili powder

1 teaspoon paprika

1 teaspoon garlic powder

1 teaspoon ground cumin

¼ teaspoon ground allspice

⅛ teaspoon ground red pepper

1 Combine ketchup, brown sugar, molasses, vinegar, dry mustard, onion powder, chili powder, paprika, garlic powder, cumin, allspice and ground red pepper in medium saucepan; stir to blend. Bring to a boil over medium-high heat, stirring to dissolve sugar.

2 Reduce heat to medium-low; cover and simmer 20 minutes or until slightly thickened, stirring occasionally.

Sweet Southern Barbecue Chicken

MAKES 4 SERVINGS

2 to 3 tablespoons olive oil, divided

½ cup chopped onion

1 clove garlic, minced

½ cup packed brown sugar

1 teaspoon dry mustard

1 tablespoon honey mustard

1 tablespoon Dijon mustard

1 cup cola beverage

2 tablespoons balsamic vinegar

2 tablespoons cider vinegar

2 tablespoons Worcestershire sauce

½ cup ketchup

2 to 3 pounds boneless skinless chicken thighs

1 Heat 1 tablespoon oil in medium skillet over medium heat. Add onion and garlic; cook and stir 2 minutes. Add brown sugar and mustards; bring to a boil over medium-high heat. Reduce heat to low; simmer 20 minutes or until sauce thickens.

2 Stir in cola, balsamic vinegar, cider vinegar, Worcestershire sauce and ketchup; simmer 15 to 20 minutes or until sauce thickens. Remove from heat.

3 Heat 1 tablespoon oil in large skillet over medium-high heat. Add half of chicken; cook 5 to 7 minutes. Turn and brush with sauce; cook 5 to 7 minutes or until cooked through. Brush both sides of chicken with sauce during last 1 to 2 minutes of cooking. Remove to plate; keep warm. Repeat with remaining oil, sauce and chicken. Serve with additional sauce.

Barbecue Chicken Pizza

MAKES 4 SERVINGS

1 pound refrigerated pizza
dough

1 tablespoon olive oil

6 ounces boneless skinless
chicken breasts, cut
into strips (about
2×¼ inch)

¼ teaspoon salt

⅛ teaspoon black pepper

6 tablespoons barbecue
sauce, divided

⅔ cup shredded mozzarella
cheese, divided

½ cup shredded smoked
Gouda cheese, divided

½ small red onion, cut
vertically into ⅛-inch
slices

2 tablespoons chopped
fresh cilantro

1 Preheat oven to 450°F. Line baking sheet with parchment paper. Let dough come to room temperature.

2 Heat oil in large skillet over medium-high heat. Season chicken with salt and pepper; cook 5 minutes or just until cooked though, stirring occasionally. Remove chicken to medium bowl. Add 2 tablespoons barbecue sauce; stir to coat.

3 Roll out dough into 12-inch circle on lightly floured surface. Remove to prepared baking sheet. Spread remaining 4 tablespoons barbecue sauce over dough, leaving ½-inch border. Sprinkle with 2 tablespoons mozzarella cheese and 2 tablespoons Gouda cheese. Top with chicken and onion; sprinkle with remaining cheeses.

4 Bake 12 to 15 minutes or until crust is browned and cheeses are bubbly. Sprinkle with cilantro.

Barbecue Beef Sandwiches

MAKES 4 SERVINGS

2½ pounds boneless beef chuck roast

2 tablespoons Southwest seasoning

1 tablespoon vegetable oil

1¼ cups beef broth

2½ cups barbecue sauce, divided

4 sandwich or pretzel buns, split

1⅓ cups prepared coleslaw* (preferably vinegar based)

Vinegar-based coleslaw provides a perfect complement to the rich beef. They can often be found at the salad bar, deli counter or prepared foods section of large supermarkets.

1 Sprinkle both sides of beef with Southwest seasoning. Heat oil in Dutch oven over medium-high heat. Add beef; cook 6 minutes per side or until browned. Remove to plate.

2 Add broth; cook 2 minutes, scraping up browned bits from bottom of Dutch oven. Stir in 2 cups barbecue sauce; bring to a boil. Return beef to Dutch oven; turn to coat.

3 Reduce heat to low; cover and cook 3 to 3½ hours or until beef is fork-tender, turning beef halfway through cooking time.

4 Remove beef to large bowl; let stand until cool enough to handle. Meanwhile, cook sauce remaining in Dutch oven over high heat 10 minutes or until reduced and slightly thickened.

5 Shred beef into bite-size pieces. Stir in 1 cup reduced cooking sauce and ¼ cup barbecue sauce. Add remaining ¼ cup barbecue sauce, if desired. Fill buns with beef mixture; top with coleslaw.

Restaurant-Style Baby Back Ribs

MAKES 4 SERVINGS

1¼ cups water

1 cup white vinegar

⅔ cup packed dark brown sugar

½ cup tomato paste

1 tablespoon yellow mustard

1½ teaspoons salt

1 teaspoon liquid smoke

1 teaspoon onion powder

½ teaspoon garlic powder

½ teaspoon paprika

2 racks pork baby back ribs (3½ to 4 pounds total)

1 Combine water, vinegar, brown sugar, tomato paste, mustard, salt, liquid smoke, onion powder, garlic powder and paprika in medium saucepan; bring to a boil over medium heat. Reduce heat to medium-low; cook 40 minutes or until sauce thickens, stirring occasionally.

2 Preheat oven to 300°F. Place each rack of ribs on large sheet of heavy-duty foil. Brush some of sauce over ribs, covering completely. Fold down edges of foil tightly to seal and create packet; arrange packets on baking sheet, seam sides up.

3 Bake 2 hours. Prepare grill or preheat broiler. Carefully open packets and drain off excess liquid.

4 Brush ribs with sauce; grill or broil 5 minutes per side or until beginning to char, brushing with sauce once or twice during grilling. Serve with remaining sauce.

Cajun BBQ Beer Can Chicken

MAKES 12 SERVINGS

4 (12-ounce) cans beer or non-alcoholic malt beverage

1½ cups **Cattlemen's**® Award Winning Classic Barbecue Sauce

¾ cup Cajun spice or Southwest seasoning blend

3 whole chickens (3 to 4 pounds each)

12 sprigs fresh thyme

CAJUN BBQ SAUCE

1 cup **Cattlemen's**® Award Winning Classic Barbecue Sauce

½ cup beer or non-alcoholic malt beverage

¼ cup butter

1 tablespoon Cajun spice or Southwest seasoning blend

1 Combine *1 can* beer, *1½ cups* barbecue sauce and *½ cup* spice blend. Following manufacturer's instructions, fill marinade injection needle with marinade. Inject chickens in several places at least 1-inch deep. Place chickens into resealable plastic food storage bags. Pour any remaining marinade over chickens. Seal bag; marinate in refrigerator 1 to 3 hours or overnight.

2 Meanwhile, prepare Cajun BBQ Sauce: In saucepan, combine *1 cup* barbecue sauce, *½ cup* beer, butter and *1 tablespoon* spice blend. Simmer 5 minutes. Refrigerate and warm just before serving.

3 Open remaining cans of beer. Spill out about *½ cup* beer from each can. Using can opener, punch several holes in tops of cans. Spoon about *1 tablespoon* additional spice blend and *4 sprigs* thyme into each can. Place 1 can upright into each cavity of chicken, arranging legs forward so chicken stands upright.

4 Place chickens upright over indirect heat on barbecue grill. Cook on a covered grill on medium-high (350°F), about 1½ hours until thigh meat registers 180°F internal temperature. (Cover chickens with foil if they become too brown while cooking.) Let stand 10 minutes before serving. Using tongs, carefully remove cans from chicken. Cut into quarters to serve. Serve with Cajun BBQ Sauce.

Pulled Pork with Honey-Chipotle Barbecue Sauce

MAKES 8 SERVINGS

1 tablespoon chili powder, divided

1 teaspoon chipotle chili powder, divided

1 teaspoon ground cumin, divided

1 teaspoon garlic powder, divided

1 teaspoon salt

1 bone-in pork shoulder (3½ pounds), trimmed

1 can (15 ounces) tomato sauce

5 tablespoons honey, divided

SLOW COOKER DIRECTIONS

1 Coat inside of slow cooker with nonstick cooking spray. Combine 1 teaspoon chili powder, ½ teaspoon chipotle chili powder, ½ teaspoon cumin, ½ teaspoon garlic powder and salt in small bowl. Rub pork with chili powder mixture. Place pork in slow cooker.

2 Combine tomato sauce, 4 tablespoons honey, remaining 2 teaspoons chili powder, ½ teaspoon chipotle chili powder, ½ teaspoon cumin and ½ teaspoon garlic powder in large bowl. Pour tomato mixture over pork in slow cooker. Cover; cook on LOW 8 hours.

3 Remove pork to large bowl; cover loosely with foil. *Turn slow cooker to HIGH.* Cover; cook on HIGH 30 minutes or until sauce is thickened. Stir in remaining 1 tablespoon honey. Turn off heat.

4 Remove bone from pork and discard. Shred pork using two forks. Stir shredded pork back into slow cooker to coat well with sauce.

Citrus Barbecue Chicken ▶

MAKES 5 SERVINGS

★ ★ ★ ★ ★ ★ ★ ★ ★ ★ ★ ★ ★ ★ ★ ★ ★ ★ ★ ★

½ cup barbecue sauce

1 teaspoon grated orange peel

1 teaspoon grated fresh ginger

5 boneless skinless chicken breasts

1 can (20 oz.) DOLE® Pineapple Slices

- **Stir** together barbecue sauce, orange peel and ginger in small bowl.

- **Grill** or broil chicken breasts 8 minutes, brushing with half of sauce. Turn chicken over and add pineapple slices to grill. Brush chicken and pineapple with remaining sauce. Continue grilling 8 to 10 minutes or until chicken is no longer pink in center and slices are lightly browned. Serve with broccoli florets and rice, if desired.

Bold and Zesty Beef Back Ribs

MAKES 5 TO 6 SERVINGS

★ ★ ★ ★ ★ ★ ★ ★ ★ ★ ★ ★ ★ ★ ★ ★ ★ ★ ★ ★

5 pounds beef back ribs, cut into 3- or 4-rib pieces

Salt and black pepper

1 teaspoon vegetable oil

1 small onion, minced

2 cloves garlic, minced

1 cup ketchup

½ cup chili sauce

2 tablespoons lemon juice

1 tablespoon packed brown sugar

1 teaspoon hot pepper sauce

1 Place ribs in shallow pan; season with salt and black pepper. Refrigerate until ready to grill.

2 For sauce, heat oil in medium saucepan over medium heat. Add onion and garlic; cook and stir 5 minutes or until onion is tender. Stir in ketchup, chili sauce, lemon juice, brown sugar and hot pepper sauce. Reduce heat to medium-low. Cook 15 minutes, stirring occasionally.

3 Meanwhile, prepare grill for indirect cooking.

4 Place ribs on grid directly over drip pan. Baste ribs generously with some of sauce. Grill, covered, 45 to 60 minutes or until ribs are tender and browned, turning occasionally.

5 Bring remaining sauce to a boil over medium-high heat; boil 1 minute. Serve ribs with sauce.

Backyard Barbecue Burgers

MAKES 6 SERVINGS

1½ pounds ground beef

5 tablespoons barbecue sauce, divided

1 onion, cut into thick slices

1 tomato, sliced

2 tablespoons olive oil

6 Kaiser rolls, split

6 leaves green or red leaf lettuce

1 Prepare grill for direct cooking. Combine beef and 2 tablespoons barbecue sauce in large bowl. Shape into six (1-inch-thick) patties.

2 Grill patties, covered, over medium heat 8 to 10 minutes (or uncovered 13 to 15 minutes) to medium (160°F) or to desired doneness, turning occasionally. Brush both sides with remaining 3 tablespoons barbecue sauce during last 5 minutes of cooking.

3 Meanwhile, brush onion* and tomato slices with oil. Grill onion slices 10 minutes and tomato slices 2 to 3 minutes.

4 Just before serving, place rolls, cut side down, on grid; grill until lightly toasted. Serve burgers on rolls with onion, tomato and lettuce.

*Onion slices may be cooked on the stovetop. Heat 2 tablespoons oil in large skillet over medium heat. Add onions; cook 10 minutes or until tender and slightly browned, stirring frequently.

BBQ Glazed Turkey a la Orange

MAKES 8 SERVINGS

1 whole turkey
   (12 to 14 pounds)
2 tablespoons olive oil
   Salt and black pepper
1 orange, cut into quarters
6 sprigs fresh thyme
2 large disposable
   aluminum foil pans
   Honey BBQ Orange Glaze
   (recipe follows)

1 Rub turkey with oil; season with salt and pepper. Place orange and thyme into cavity. Tie legs together and tuck wing tips underneath. Place turkey on rack in doubled foil pan. Set on grill.

2 Grill turkey, covered, over indirect medium heat (325°F) for 11 to 14 minutes per pound or until meat thermometer inserted into turkey thigh reaches 180°F. Baste turkey with some of the Honey BBQ Orange Glaze during last 30 minutes of cooking. Reserve remaining glaze.

3 Remove turkey to platter. Discard orange and thyme from cavity. Loosely tent with foil and let rest 15 minutes before carving. Heat reserved Honey BBQ Orange Glaze and serve with turkey.

Honey BBQ Orange Glaze

MAKES ABOUT 1½ CUPS

1 cup *Cattlemen's*® Golden
   Honey Barbecue Sauce
¼ cup orange-flavor liqueur
   or orange juice
¼ cup butter
1 tablespoon grated orange
   zest
2 teaspoons minced fresh
   thyme leaves

Place all ingredients in small saucepan. Simmer until butter melts, flavors are blended and sauce thickens slightly.

Grilled Pork Chops
with Lager Barbecue Sauce

MAKES 4 SERVINGS

1 cup lager

⅓ cup maple syrup

3 tablespoons molasses

1 teaspoon Mexican-style hot chili powder

4 bone-in, center-cut pork chops, 1 inch thick (2 to 2¼ pounds)

Lager Barbecue Sauce (recipe follows)

¾ teaspoon salt

¼ teaspoon black pepper

1 Combine lager, maple syrup, molasses, chili powder and pork chops in large resealable food storage bag. Marinate in refrigerator 2 hours, turning occasionally. Prepare Lager Barbecue Sauce.

2 Prepare grill for direct cooking over medium-high heat. Oil grid.

3 Remove pork chops from marinade; discard marinade. Sprinkle with salt and pepper. Grill 6 to 7 minutes per side or until 160°F. Serve with Lager Barbecue Sauce.

Lager Barbecue Sauce

MAKES ABOUT ½ CUP

½ cup lager

⅓ cup ketchup

3 tablespoons maple syrup

2 tablespoons finely chopped onion

1 tablespoon molasses

1 tablespoon cider vinegar

½ teaspoon Mexican-style hot chili powder

Combine lager, ketchup, maple syrup, onion, molasses, vinegar and chili powder in small saucepan over medium heat. Bring to a gentle simmer and cook, stirring occasionally, 10 to 12 minutes or until slightly thickened.

Carolina-Style Barbecue Chicken

MAKES 8 SERVINGS

2 **pounds boneless skinless chicken breasts**

¾ **cup packed light brown sugar, divided**

¾ **cup FRENCH'S® Classic Yellow® Mustard**

½ **cup cider vinegar**

¼ **cup FRANK'S RedHot® Original Cayenne Pepper Sauce**

2 **tablespoons vegetable oil**

2 **tablespoons FRENCH'S® Worcestershire Sauce**

½ **teaspoon salt**

¼ **teaspoon black pepper**

1 Place chicken in large resealable plastic food storage bag. Combine ½ cup brown sugar, mustard, vinegar, **FRANK'S RedHot®** Sauce, oil, Worcestershire, salt and pepper in 4-cup measure; mix well. Pour 1 cup mustard mixture over chicken. Seal bag; marinate in refrigerator 1 hour or overnight.

2 Pour remaining mustard mixture into small saucepan. Stir in remaining ¼ cup brown sugar. Bring to a boil. Reduce heat; simmer 5 minutes or until sugar dissolves and mixture thickens slightly, stirring often. Reserve for serving sauce.

3 Place chicken on well-oiled grid, reserving marinade. Grill over high heat 10 to 15 minutes or until chicken is no longer pink in center, turning and basting once with marinade. *Do not baste during last 5 minutes of cooking.* Discard any remaining marinade. Serve chicken with reserved sauce.

SOUPS, STEWS AND CHILI

Five-Way Cincinnati Chili

MAKES 6 SERVINGS

- 1 pound uncooked spaghetti, broken in half
- 1 pound ground beef chuck
- 2 cans (10 ounces each) tomatoes and green chiles, undrained
- 1 can (15 ounces) red kidney beans, drained
- 1 can (10½ ounces) condensed French onion soup, undiluted
- 1¼ cups water
- 1 tablespoon chili powder
- 1 teaspoon sugar
- ½ teaspoon salt
- ¼ teaspoon ground cinnamon
- ½ cup chopped onion
- ½ cup (2 ounces) shredded Cheddar cheese

1 Cook pasta according to package directions; drain.

2 Meanwhile, brown beef in large saucepan or Dutch oven over medium-high heat 6 to 8 minutes or until browned, stirring to break up meat. Drain fat. Add tomatoes, beans, soup, water, chili powder, sugar, salt and cinnamon to saucepan; bring to a boil. Reduce heat to low. Simmer, uncovered, 10 minutes, stirring occasionally.

3 Serve chili over spaghetti; sprinkle with onion and cheese.

COOK'S NOTES

Serve this traditional chili your way or one of the ways Cincinnatians do—two-way over spaghetti, three-way with cheese, four-way with cheese and chopped onion or five-way with beans added to the chili.

Cape Cod Stew

MAKES 8 SERVINGS

- 2 pounds medium raw shrimp, peeled and deveined
- 2 pounds fresh cod or other white fish
- 3 lobsters (1½ to 2½ pounds *each*), uncooked
- 1 pound mussels or clams, scrubbed
- 2 cans (about 14 ounces *each*) chopped tomatoes
- 4 cups beef broth
- ½ cup chopped onion
- ½ cup chopped carrot
- ½ cup chopped fresh cilantro
- 2 tablespoons sea salt
- 2 teaspoons minced garlic
- 2 teaspoons lemon juice
- 4 bay leaves
- 1 teaspoon dried thyme
- ½ teaspoon saffron threads

1 Cut shrimp and fish into bite-size pieces and place in large bowl; refrigerate. Remove lobster tails and claws. Chop tail into 2-inch pieces and separate claws at joints. Place lobster and mussels in large bowl; refrigerate.

2 Combine tomatoes, broth, onion, carrot, cilantro, salt, garlic, lemon juice, bay leaves, thyme and saffron in **Crockpot®** slow cooker; stir to blend. Cover; cook on LOW 7 hours.

3 Add seafood. Turn **Crockpot®** slow cooker to HIGH. Cover; cook on HIGH 45 minutes to 1 hour or until seafood is just cooked through. Remove and discard bay leaves. Discard any mussels that do not open.

New Orleans Fish Soup

MAKES 4 SERVINGS

1 can (about 15 ounces) cannellini beans, rinsed and drained

1 can (about 14 ounces) chicken broth

1 yellow squash, halved lengthwise and sliced (1 cup)

1 tablespoon Cajun seasoning

2 cans (about 14 ounces each) stewed tomatoes

1 pound skinless firm fish fillets, such as grouper, cod or haddock, cut into 1-inch pieces

½ cup sliced green onions

1 teaspoon grated orange peel

1 Combine beans, broth, squash and Cajun seasoning in large saucepan; bring to a boil over high heat.

2 Stir in tomatoes and fish. Reduce heat to medium-low; cover and simmer 3 to 5 minutes or until fish begins to flake when tested with fork. Stir in green onions and orange peel.

Smokin' Texas Chili

MAKES 6 SERVINGS

- 2 tablespoons olive oil
- 1½ pounds boneless beef sirloin steak **or** top round steak, ¾-inch thick, cut into ½-inch pieces
- 1 medium onion, chopped (about ½ cup)
- 2 cloves garlic, minced
- 3 cups Pace® Picante Sauce
- ½ cup water
- 1 tablespoon chili powder
- 1 teaspoon ground cumin
- 1 can (about 15 ounces) red kidney beans, rinsed and drained
- ¼ cup chopped fresh cilantro leaves
- Chili Toppings

1 Heat **1 tablespoon** oil in a 6-quart saucepot over medium-high heat. Add the beef in 2 batches and cook until it's well browned, stirring often. Remove the beef from the saucepot.

2 Add the remaining oil and heat over medium heat. Add the onion and cook until it's tender. Add the garlic and cook for 30 seconds.

3 Add the picante sauce, water, chili powder and cumin. Heat to a boil. Return the beef to the saucepot. Stir in the beans. Reduce the heat to low. Cover and cook for 1 hour. Uncover and cook for 30 minutes or until the beef is fork-tender.

4 Sprinkle with the cilantro and Chili Toppings, if desired.

CHILI TOPPINGS

Chopped tomatoes, chopped onions, sour cream and/or shredded cheese.

Northwest Beef and Vegetable Soup

MAKES 6 TO 8 SERVINGS

2 tablespoons olive oil

1 pound cubed beef stew meat

1 onion, chopped

1 clove garlic, minced

8 cups water

3½ cups canned crushed tomatoes, undrained

1 butternut squash, cut into 1-inch pieces

1 can (about 15 ounces) cannellini beans, rinsed and drained

1 turnip, peeled and cut into 1-inch pieces

1 large potato, cut into 1-inch pieces

2 stalks celery, sliced

2 tablespoons minced fresh basil

1½ teaspoons salt

1 teaspoon black pepper

1 Heat oil in large skillet over medium heat. Add beef; cook and stir 6 to 8 minutes or until browned on all sides. Add onion and garlic during last few minutes of browning. Remove to **Crockpot**® slow cooker.

2 Add water, tomatoes, squash, beans, turnip, potato, celery, basil, salt and pepper; stir to blend. Cover; cook on HIGH 2 hours. Turn **Crockpot**® slow cooker to LOW. Cover; cook on LOW 4 to 6 hours.

Beer and Cheese Soup

MAKES 4 SERVINGS

1 can (about 14 ounces) chicken broth

1 cup beer

¼ cup finely chopped onion

2 cloves garlic, minced

¾ teaspoon dried thyme

1½ cups (6 ounces) shredded American cheese

1½ cups (6 ounces) shredded sharp Cheddar cheese

1 cup milk

½ teaspoon paprika

2 to 3 slices pumpernickel or rye bread

SLOW COOKER DIRECTIONS

1 Combine broth, beer, onion, garlic and thyme in slow cooker. Cover; cook on LOW 4 hours.

2 *Turn slow cooker to HIGH.* Stir in cheeses, milk and paprika. Cover; cook on HIGH 45 to 60 minutes or until heated through.

3 Meanwhile, preheat oven to 425°F. Cut bread into ½-inch cubes; place on small baking sheet. Bake 10 to 12 minutes or until crisp, stirring once. Serve croutons with soup.

Broccoli Cheddar Soup

MAKES 6 SERVINGS

3 tablespoons butter

1 medium onion, chopped

3 tablespoons all-purpose flour

¼ teaspoon ground nutmeg

¼ teaspoon black pepper

4 cups vegetable broth

1 large bunch broccoli, chopped

1 medium red potato, peeled and chopped

1 teaspoon salt

1 bay leaf

1½ cups (6 ounces) shredded Cheddar cheese, plus additional for garnish

½ cup whipping cream

SLOW COOKER DIRECTIONS

1 Melt butter in medium saucepan over medium heat. Add onion; cook and stir 6 minutes or until softened. Add flour, nutmeg and pepper; cook and stir 1 minute. Remove to slow cooker. Stir in broth, broccoli, potato, salt and bay leaf.

2 Cover; cook on HIGH 3 hours. Remove and discard bay leaf. Add soup in batches to food processor or blender; purée until desired consistency. Pour soup back into slow cooker. Stir in 1½ cups cheese and cream until cheese is melted. Garnish with additional cheese.

White Chicken Chili

MAKES 6 TO 8 SERVINGS

8 ounces dried navy beans, rinsed and sorted

1 tablespoon vegetable oil

2 pounds boneless skinless chicken breasts (about 4)

2 onions, chopped

1 tablespoon minced garlic

2 teaspoons ground cumin

2 teaspoons salt

1 teaspoon dried oregano

¼ teaspoon black pepper

¼ teaspoon ground red pepper (optional)

4 cups chicken broth

1 can (4 ounces) fire-roasted diced mild green chiles, rinsed and drained

¼ cup chopped fresh cilantro

SLOW COOKER DIRECTIONS

1 Place beans in bottom of slow cooker. Heat oil in large skillet over medium-high heat. Add chicken; cook 8 minutes or until browned on all sides. Remove to slow cooker.

2 Heat same skillet over medium heat. Add onions; cook 6 minutes or until softened and lightly browned. Add garlic, cumin, salt, oregano, black pepper and ground red pepper, if desired; cook and stir 1 minute. Add broth and chiles; bring to a simmer, stirring to scrape up any browned bits from bottom of skillet. Remove onion mixture to slow cooker.

3 Cover; cook on LOW 5 hours. Remove chicken to large cutting board; shred with two forks. Return chicken to slow cooker. Top each serving with cilantro.

Baked Potato Soup

MAKES 6 TO 8 SERVINGS

- 3 medium russet potatoes (about 1 pound)
- ¼ cup (½ stick) butter
- 1 cup chopped onion
- ½ cup all-purpose flour
- 4 cups chicken or vegetable broth
- 1½ cups instant mashed potato flakes
- 1 cup water
- 1 cup half-and-half
- 1 teaspoon salt
- ½ teaspoon dried basil
- ½ teaspoon dried thyme
- ¼ teaspoon black pepper
- 1 cup (4 ounces) shredded Cheddar cheese
- 4 slices bacon, crisp-cooked and crumbled
- 1 green onion, chopped

1. Preheat oven to 400°F. Scrub potatoes and prick in several places with fork. Place in baking pan; bake 1 hour. Cool completely; peel and cut into ½-inch cubes. (Potatoes can be prepared several days in advance; refrigerate until ready to use.)

2. Melt butter in large saucepan or Dutch oven over medium heat. Add onion; cook and stir 3 minutes or until softened. Whisk in flour; cook and stir 1 minute. Gradually whisk in broth until well blended. Stir in mashed potato flakes, water, half-and-half, salt, basil, thyme and pepper; bring to a boil over medium-high heat. Reduce heat to medium; cook 5 minutes.

3. Stir in baked potato cubes; cook 10 to 15 minutes or until soup is thickened and heated through. Ladle into bowls; top with cheese, bacon and green onion.

Chicken Noodle Soup

MAKES 8 SERVINGS

2 tablespoons butter

1 cup chopped onion

1 cup sliced carrots

½ cup diced celery

2 tablespoons vegetable oil

1 pound chicken breast tenderloins

1 pound chicken thigh fillets

4 cups chicken broth, divided

2 cups water

1 tablespoon minced fresh parsley, plus additional for garnish

1½ teaspoons salt

½ teaspoon black pepper

3 cups uncooked egg noodles

1 Melt butter in large saucepan or Dutch oven over medium-low heat. Add onion, carrots and celery; cook 8 minutes or until vegetables are soft, stirring occasionally.

2 Meanwhile, heat oil in large skillet over medium-high heat. Add chicken in single layer; cook 12 minutes or until lightly browned and cooked through, turning once. Remove chicken to large cutting board. Add 1 cup broth to skillet; cook 1 minute, scraping up browned bits from bottom of skillet. Add broth to vegetables in saucepan. Stir in remaining 3 cups broth, water, 1 tablespoon parsley, salt and pepper.

3 Chop chicken into 1-inch pieces when cool enough to handle. Add to soup; bring to a boil over medium-high heat. Reduce heat to medium-low; cook 15 minutes. Add noodles; cook 15 minutes or until noodles are tender. Ladle into bowls; garnish with additional parsley.

Corn Chip Chili

MAKES 6 SERVINGS

- 1 tablespoon olive oil
- 1 medium onion, chopped
- 1 medium red bell pepper, chopped
- 1 jalapeño pepper, seeded and finely chopped
- 4 cloves garlic, minced
- 2 pounds ground beef
- 1 can (4 ounces) diced green chiles, drained
- 2 cans (about 14 ounces each) fire-roasted diced tomatoes
- 2 tablespoons chili powder
- 1½ teaspoons ground cumin
- 1½ teaspoons dried oregano
- ¾ teaspoon salt
- 3 cups corn chips
- 1 cup (4 ounces) shredded sharp Cheddar cheese
- 6 tablespoons chopped green onions

SLOW COOKER DIRECTIONS

1 Coat inside of slow cooker with nonstick cooking spray.

2 Heat oil in large skillet over medium-high heat. Add onion, bell pepper, jalapeño pepper and garlic; cook and stir 3 minutes or until softened. Add beef; cook and stir 10 to 12 minutes or until beef is no longer pink and liquid has evaporated. Stir in green chiles; cook 1 minute. Remove beef mixture to slow cooker. Stir in tomatoes, chili powder, cumin, oregano and salt.

3 Cover; cook on LOW 6 to 7 hours or on HIGH 3 to 3½ hours. Place corn chips evenly into serving bowls; top with chili. Sprinkle with cheese and green onions.

Harvest Pumpkin Soup

MAKES 8 SERVINGS

- 1 sugar pumpkin or acorn squash (about 2 pounds)
- 1 kabocha or butternut squash (about 2 pounds)
  Salt and black pepper
- 2 tablespoons olive oil
- 2 tablespoons butter
- 1 large onion, finely chopped
- 2 stalks celery, chopped
- 1 medium carrot, chopped
- ¼ cup packed brown sugar
- 2 tablespoons tomato paste
- 1 tablespoon minced fresh ginger
- 1 clove garlic, minced
- 1 teaspoon salt
- 1 teaspoon ground cinnamon
- ¼ teaspoon ground cumin
- ¼ teaspoon black pepper
- 4 cups vegetable broth
- 1 cup milk
- 2 teaspoons lemon juice
  Roasted pumpkin seeds (optional, see Tip)

1 Preheat oven to 400°F. Line large baking sheet with foil; spray with nonstick cooking spray.

2 Cut pumpkin and kabocha squash in half; remove and discard seeds and strings or use seeds for garnish (see Tip). Season cut sides with salt and pepper. Place cut sides down on prepared baking sheet; bake 30 to 45 minutes or until fork-tender. When squash is cool enough to handle, remove skin; chop flesh into 1-inch pieces.

3 Heat oil and butter in large saucepan or Dutch oven over medium-high heat. Add onion, celery and carrot; cook and stir 5 minutes or until vegetables are tender. Add brown sugar, tomato paste, ginger, garlic, 1 teaspoon salt, cinnamon, cumin and ¼ teaspoon pepper; cook and stir 1 minute. Stir in broth and squash; bring to a boil. Reduce heat to medium; cook 20 minutes or until squash is very soft.

4 Blend soup with hand-held immersion blender until desired consistency. (Or process in batches in food processor or blender.) Stir in milk and lemon juice; cook until heated through. Garnish with pumpkin seeds.

TIP

Roasted pumpkin seeds can be found at many supermarkets, or you can roast the seeds that you remove from the pumpkin (and the squash) in the recipe. Combine the seeds with 1 teaspoon vegetable oil and ⅛ teaspoon salt in a small bowl; toss to coat. Spread in a single layer on a small foil-lined baking sheet; bake at 300°F 20 to 25 minutes or until the seeds begin to brown, stirring once.

PATRIOTIC DINNERS

Philly Cheese Steaks

MAKES 8 SERVINGS

2 pounds beef round steak, sliced

4 onions, sliced

2 green bell peppers, sliced

2 tablespoons butter, melted

1 tablespoon garlic-pepper seasoning

Salt

½ cup water

2 teaspoons beef bouillon granules

8 crusty Italian or French rolls, sliced in half*

8 slices Cheddar cheese, cut in half

*Toast rolls under broiler or on griddle, if desired.

1 Combine steak, onions, bell peppers, butter, garlic-pepper seasoning and salt in **Crockpot®** slow cooker.

2 Whisk together water and bouillon in small bowl; pour into **Crockpot®** slow cooker. Cover; cook on LOW 6 to 8 hours.

3 Remove beef, onions and bell peppers from **Crockpot®** slow cooker and pile on rolls. Top with cheese and place under broiler until cheese is melted.

Kansas City Style Ribs

MAKES 6 SERVINGS

2 sheets (18×24 inches each) REYNOLDS WRAP® Heavy Duty Foil

3 pounds baby back pork ribs

½ cup water

½ teaspoon liquid smoke

2 tablespoons butter or vegetable oil

½ cup finely chopped onion

2 cups ketchup

¼ cup Worcestershire sauce

¼ cup cider vinegar

1 tablespoon prepared mustard

1 tablespoon molasses

½ teaspoon ground cumin

PREHEAT grill to medium. Cut each rack of ribs into thirds. Center half of ribs in single layer on each sheet of REYNOLDS WRAP® Heavy Duty Aluminum Foil.

BRING up foil sides. Double fold one end to seal. Through open end, add ¼ cup water and ¼ teaspoon liquid smoke. Double fold remaining end, leaving room for heat circulation inside packet. Repeat for second packet.

GRILL 45 minutes to 1 hour on medium in covered grill. Melt butter in medium saucepan over medium-high heat. Add onion and cook until tender. Add remaining ingredients. Simmer over medium-low heat 20 to 25 minutes while ribs steam in the foil packet. Remove steamed ribs carefully from foil. Place directly on grill.

BRUSH ribs generously with sauce. Continue grilling 10 to 15 minutes on medium in uncovered grill, brushing with sauce and turning every 5 minutes to cook evenly.

Yankee Pot Roast and Vegetables

MAKES 10 TO 12 SERVINGS

1 boneless beef chuck pot roast (2½ pounds)

Salt and black pepper

3 unpeeled baking potatoes (about 1 pound), cut into quarters

2 carrots, cut into ¾-inch slices

2 stalks celery, cut into ¾-inch slices

1 onion, sliced

1 parsnip, cut into ¾-inch slices

2 bay leaves

1 teaspoon dried rosemary

½ teaspoon dried thyme

½ cup beef broth

SLOW COOKER DIRECTIONS

1 Trim and discard excess fat from beef. Cut into ¾-inch pieces; sprinkle with salt and pepper.

2 Combine potatoes, carrots, celery, onion, parsnip, bay leaves, rosemary and thyme in slow cooker. Top with beef. Pour broth over beef. Cover; cook on LOW 8½ to 9 hours or until beef is fork-tender.

3 Remove beef and vegetables to serving platter. Remove and discard bay leaves.

NOTE

To make gravy, ladle the juices into a 2-cup measure; let stand 5 minutes. Skim off fat. Measure remaining juices and heat to a boil in small saucepan. For each cup of juices, mix 2 tablespoons flour with ¼ cup cold water in small bowl until smooth; add to boiling juices. Cook and stir constantly 1 minute or until thickened.

Steamed Maryland Crabs

MAKES 4 SERVINGS

2 cups beer or water

2 cups cider vinegar or white vinegar

2 dozen live Maryland blue crabs

1 cup seafood seasoning

Two dozen crabs will yield about 2½ cups cleaned crab meat.

1 Pour beer and vinegar into large stockpot. Place steaming rack in bottom of pot. Place half of crabs on rack. Sprinkle half of seasoning over crabs. Repeat layers with remaining crabs and seasoning.

2 Cover; cook over high heat until liquid begins to steam. Steam about 25 minutes or until crabs turn red and meat is white. Remove crabs to large serving platter, using tongs.

TO SERVE

Cover table with disposable paper cloth or newspaper.

To pick crabs, place each on its back. With thumb, pry off "apron" flap (the "pull tab"-looking shell in the center) and discard.

Lift off top shell and discard. With knife edge, scrape off 6 gills (lungs) on either side of the body.

The yellow or reddish-brown material behind the mouth area is the fat, heart and/or crab roe and is edible. Discard the mouth area.

Hold crab at each side; break apart at center. Discard legs. Remove membrane cover with knife, exposing large chunks of meat; remove with fingers or knife.

Crack claws with mallet or knife handle to expose meat.

Coney Island Chili Dog Tacos

MAKES 8 SERVINGS

- 1 tablespoon olive oil
- 8 hot dogs
- 1¼ pounds 90% extra lean ground beef
- 1 tablespoon chili powder
- 1 jar (16 ounces) Pace® Chunky Salsa-Mild
- 8 flour tortillas (6-inch) **or** taco shells, warmed
- 1 medium onion, diced (about ½ cup)
- ½ cup shredded Cheddar cheese

1 Heat the oil in a 12-inch skillet over medium-high heat. Add the hot dogs and cook until browned. Remove the hot dogs, cover and keep warm.

2 Cook the beef and chili powder in the skillet until the beef is well browned, stirring often to separate meat. Pour off any fat. Stir in the salsa. Reduce the heat to low. Cook for 5 minutes, stirring occasionally.

3 Place 1 hot dog into each tortilla. Top with the beef mixture, onion and cheese.

PREP AHEAD

You can prepare the beef mixture, cool it completely, then place into a resealable freezer bag (remove all air), seal the bag and refrigerate for up to 3 days. Or, freeze for up to 3 months and thaw overnight in the refrigerator before reheating. Reheat in the skillet after cooking the hot dogs as shown.

SERVING SUGGESTION

Try topping these chili dogs with a drizzle of yellow mustard!

Simple Roasted Chicken

MAKES 4 SERVINGS

1 whole chicken (about 4 pounds)

3 tablespoons butter, softened

1½ teaspoons salt

1 teaspoon onion powder

1 teaspoon dried thyme

½ teaspoon garlic powder

½ teaspoon paprika

½ teaspoon black pepper

Fresh parsley sprigs and lemon wedges (optional)

1 Preheat oven to 425°F. Pat chicken dry; place in small baking dish or on baking sheet.

2 Combine butter, salt, onion powder, thyme, garlic powder, paprika and pepper in small microwavable bowl; mash with fork until well blended. Loosen skin on breasts and thighs; spread about one third of butter mixture under skin.

3 Microwave remaining butter mixture until melted. Brush melted butter mixture all over outside of chicken and inside cavity. Tie drumsticks together with kitchen string and tuck wing tips under.

4 Roast 20 minutes. *Reduce oven temperature to 375°F.* Roast 45 to 55 minutes or until chicken is cooked through (165°F), basting once with pan juices during last 10 minutes of cooking time. Remove chicken to large cutting board; tent with foil. Let stand 15 minutes before carving. Garnish with parsley and lemon wedges.

BLT Supreme ▶

MAKES 2 SERVINGS

- 6 to 8 slices thick-cut bacon
- ⅓ cup mayonnaise
- 1½ teaspoons minced chipotle pepper in adobo sauce
- 1 teaspoon lime juice
- 1 ripe avocado
- ⅛ teaspoon salt
- ⅛ teaspoon black pepper
- 4 leaves romaine lettuce
- ½ baguette, cut into 2 (8-inch) lengths *or* 2 hoagie rolls, split and toasted
- 6 to 8 slices tomato

1 Cook bacon in skillet or oven until crisp-chewy. Drain on paper towel-lined plate.

2 Meanwhile, combine mayonnaise, chipotle pepper and lime juice in small bowl; mix well. Coarsely mash avocado in another small bowl; stir in salt and black pepper. Cut romaine leaves crosswise into ¼-inch strips.

3 For each sandwich, spread heaping tablespoon mayonnaise mixture on bottom half of baguette; top with one fourth of lettuce. Arrange 3 to 4 slices bacon over lettuce; spread 2 tablespoons mashed avocado over bacon. Drizzle with heaping tablespoon mayonnaise mixture. Top with 3 to 4 tomato slices, one fourth of lettuce and 3 to 4 slices bacon. Close sandwich with top half of baguette.

Chili and Cheese "Baked" Potato Supper

MAKES 4 SERVINGS

- 4 russet potatoes (about 2 pounds)
- 2 cups prepared chili
- ½ cup (2 ounces) shredded Cheddar cheese
- 4 tablespoons sour cream (optional)
- 2 green onions, sliced

SLOW COOKER DIRECTIONS

1 Prick potatoes in several places with fork. Wrap potatoes in foil. Place in slow cooker. Cover; cook on LOW 8 to 10 hours or on HIGH 4 to 5 hours. Carefully unwrap potatoes and place on serving dish.

2 Heat chili in microwave or on stovetop. Split hot potatoes and spoon chili on top. Sprinkle with cheese, sour cream, if desired, and green onions.

Cheeseburger Potato Casserole

MAKES 6 SERVINGS

1 pound ground beef

½ cup chopped onion

1 can (about 10¾ ounces) Cheddar cheese soup

¼ cup sweet pickle relish

2 tablespoons brown mustard

2 tablespoons ketchup, plus additional for topping

1 tablespoon Worcestershire sauce

1 package (30 ounces) shredded potatoes

2 cups (8 ounces) shredded Cheddar cheese

1 teaspoon salt

½ teaspoon black pepper

Chopped green onions (optional)

SLOW COOKER DIRECTIONS

1 Coat inside of slow cooker with nonstick cooking spray. Brown beef and onion in large skillet over medium-high heat 6 to 8 minutes, stirring to break up meat. Drain fat. Stir in cheese soup, relish, mustard, 2 tablespoons ketchup and Worcestershire sauce until well blended.

2 Arrange half of potatoes in bottom of slow cooker. Spoon half of meat mixture over potatoes. Sprinkle with 1½ cups cheese, ½ teaspoon salt and ¼ teaspoon pepper. Top with remaining half of potatoes. Add remaining half of meat mixture; sprinkle with remaining ½ cup cheese, ½ teaspoon salt and ¼ teaspoon pepper. Cover; cook on LOW 4 hours or on HIGH 2 hours. Top with additional ketchup and green onions, if desired.

Broiled Cajun Fish Fillets

MAKES 4 SERVINGS

- 2 tablespoons all-purpose flour
- ½ cup seasoned dry bread crumbs
- 1 teaspoon dried thyme
- ½ teaspoon garlic salt
- ¼ teaspoon ground red pepper
- ¼ teaspoon black pepper
- 1 egg
- 1 tablespoon milk or water
- 4 scrod or orange roughy fillets, ½ inch thick (4 to 5 ounces each)
- 2 tablespoons butter, melted, divided
- ⅓ cup regular mayonnaise
- 2 tablespoons sweet pickle relish
- 1 tablespoon lemon juice
- 1 teaspoon prepared horseradish

1 Preheat broiler. Spray baking sheet with nonstick cooking spray.

2 Place flour in large resealable food storage bag. Combine bread crumbs, thyme, garlic salt, red pepper and black pepper in second bag. Beat egg and milk in shallow dish. Place each fillet, one at a time, in flour; shake bag to coat lightly. Dip fillets into egg mixture, letting excess drip off. Place fillets in bread crumb mixture; shake to coat well. Transfer fillets to prepared baking sheet. Brush fish with 1 tablespoon butter.

3 Broil 4 to 5 inches from heat 3 minutes. Turn fish; brush with remaining 1 tablespoon butter; broil 3 minutes or until fish begins to flake when tested with fork.

4 Meanwhile, combine mayonnaise, relish, juice and horseradish in small bowl; mix well. Serve sauce with fish.

CUTTING CORNERS

You can prepare the tartar sauce in advance. Cover and refrigerate up to 1 day before serving. Then all you need to do is stir lightly before serving. Or, substitute your favorite prepared tartar sauce.

Gourmet Burgers with Pancetta and Gorgonzola

MAKES 4 SERVINGS

1½ pounds ground beef

1 cup (4 ounces) gorgonzola or blue cheese crumbles

2 tablespoons mayonnaise

1 red bell pepper, quartered

4 thick slices red onion

Salt and black pepper

4 egg or brioche rolls, split and toasted

Oak leaf or baby romaine lettuce

4 to 8 slices pancetta or bacon, crisp-cooked

1 Prepare grill for direct cooking. Shape beef into four patties about ¾ inch thick. Cover and refrigerate. Combine cheese and mayonnaise in small bowl; refrigerate until ready to serve.

2 Grill bell pepper and onion, covered, over medium-high heat 8 to 10 minutes or until browned, turning once. (Use grill basket, if desired.) Remove to plate; keep warm.

3 Place patties on grid over medium heat. Grill, covered, 8 to 10 minutes (or uncovered, 13 to 15 minutes) to medium (160°F) or to desired doneness, turning occasionally. Season with salt and black pepper.

4 Spread cheese mixture on cut surfaces of rolls. Top bottom half of each roll with lettuce, burger, pancetta, onion, bell pepper and top half of roll.

Meatloaf

MAKES 6 TO 8 SERVINGS

- 1 tablespoon vegetable oil
- 2 green onions, minced
- ¼ cup minced green bell pepper
- ¼ cup grated carrot
- 3 cloves garlic, minced
- ¾ cup milk
- 2 eggs, beaten
- 1 pound ground beef
- 1 pound ground pork
- 1 cup plain dry bread crumbs
- 2 teaspoons salt
- ½ teaspoon onion powder
- ½ teaspoon black pepper
- ½ cup ketchup, divided

1 Preheat oven to 350°F.

2 Heat oil in large skillet over medium-high heat. Add green onions, bell pepper, carrot and garlic; cook and stir 5 minutes or until vegetables are softened.

3 Whisk milk and eggs in medium bowl until well blended. Gently mix beef, pork, bread crumbs, salt, onion powder and black pepper in large bowl with hands. Add milk mixture, vegetables and ¼ cup ketchup; mix gently. Press into 9×5-inch loaf pan; place pan on rimmed baking sheet.

4 Bake 30 minutes. Spread remaining ¼ cup ketchup over meatloaf; bake 1 hour or until cooked through (160°F). Cool in pan 10 minutes; cut into slices.

Lemon Garlic Roast Chicken

MAKES 4 SERVINGS

4 sprigs fresh rosemary, divided

6 cloves garlic, divided

1 lemon

2 tablespoons butter, softened

2 teaspoons salt, divided

2 large russet potatoes, cut into ¾-inch pieces

2 onions, cut into 1-inch pieces

2 tablespoons olive oil

½ teaspoon black pepper

1 whole chicken (3 to 4 pounds)

1 Preheat oven to 400°F. Finely chop 2 sprigs rosemary (about 2 tablespoons). Mince 3 cloves garlic. Grate peel from lemon. Combine butter, chopped rosemary, minced garlic, lemon peel and ½ teaspoon salt in small bowl; mix well. Set aside while preparing vegetables.

2 Combine potatoes, onions, oil, 1 teaspoon salt and ½ teaspoon pepper in medium bowl; toss to coat. Spread mixture in single layer in large cast iron skillet.

3 Smash remaining 3 cloves garlic. Cut lemon into quarters. Season cavity of chicken with remaining ½ teaspoon salt. Place garlic, lemon quarters and remaining 2 sprigs rosemary in cavity; tie legs with kitchen string, if desired. Place chicken on top of vegetables in skillet; spread butter mixture over chicken.

4 Roast about 1 hour or until chicken is cooked through (165°F) and potatoes are tender. Let stand 10 minutes before carving. Sprinkle with additional salt and pepper to taste.

The Royal Burger

MAKES 2 SERVINGS

ROYAL SEASONING

- 2 tablespoons salt
- 1½ tablespoons paprika
- 1 tablespoon garlic powder
- 1½ teaspoons onion powder
- 1½ teaspoons chili powder
- ¾ teaspoon ground cumin
- ¾ teaspoon dried basil
- ¾ teaspoon black pepper
- ¼ teaspoon dried oregano
- 1 teaspoon Royal Seasoning (recipe follows), divided

ROYAL BURGERS

- 4 slices bacon
- 12 ounces ground beef
- 2 slices deli American cheese
- 2 eggs
  Salt and black pepper
- 2 sesame seed buns, split and toasted
- 2 tablespoons mayonnaise
- ½ cup shredded lettuce
- 2 slices ripe tomato

1 For Royal Seasoning, combine 2 tablespoons salt, paprika, garlic powder, onion powder, chili powder, cumin, basil, ¾ teaspoon black pepper and oregano in small bowl; mix well.*

2 For Royal Burgers, cook bacon in large skillet over medium heat; drain on paper towel-lined plate. Pour off all but 1 teaspoon drippings from skillet. (Reserve some bacon drippings for frying eggs, if desired.)

3 Combine beef and ¾ teaspoon Royal Seasoning in medium bowl; mix gently. Shape into two 5-inch patties. Sprinkle both sides of patties with remaining ¼ teaspoon seasoning mix.

4 Return skillet to medium heat. Cook patties 5 minutes per side or until cooked through (160°F).** Top each burger with cheese slice during last minute of cooking.

5 While burgers are cooking, heat 2 teaspoons reserved bacon drippings or butter in another large skillet or griddle over medium heat. Crack eggs into skillet; cook 3 to 4 minutes or until whites are set and yolks begin to thicken and firm around edges. Season with salt and pepper.

6 Spread cut sides of buns with mayonnaise. Top bottom halves of buns with lettuce, burgers, bacon, tomato, eggs and top halves of buns.

Store seasoning mix in an airtight container. May also be used to season steaks, chicken and vegetables.

**Patties can also be grilled or broiled 5 minutes per side or until cooked through.*

Cornmeal-Crusted Catfish

MAKES 4 SERVINGS

½ cup cornmeal

¼ cup crushed pecans

2 teaspoons dried minced onion

1½ teaspoons garlic powder

1 teaspoon salt

1 teaspoon paprika

½ teaspoon black pepper

3 tablespoons mayonnaise

2 tablespoons apricot preserves or fruit spread

1 pound catfish fillets

1 Heat medium nonstick skillet over medium heat. Add cornmeal, pecans, onion, garlic powder, salt, paprika and pepper; cook and stir 3 minutes or until cornmeal begins to brown. Remove to shallow dish.

2 Combine mayonnaise and preserves in small bowl. Coat catfish with mayonnaise mixture. Dredge in toasted cornmeal mixture; turn to coat.

3 Spray same skillet with nonstick cooking spray; heat over medium heat. Add catfish; cook 3 to 4 minutes on each side or until fish begins to flake when tested with fork.

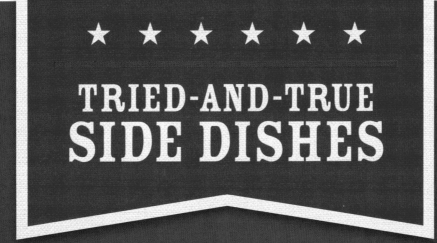

Boston Baked Beans

MAKES 4 TO 6 SERVINGS

★ ★

2 cans (about 15 ounces each) navy or Great Northern beans, rinsed and drained

½ cup beer (not dark beer)

⅓ cup finely chopped onion

⅓ cup ketchup

3 tablespoons light molasses

2 teaspoons Worcestershire sauce

1 teaspoon dry mustard

½ teaspoon ground ginger

4 slices bacon

1 Preheat oven to 350°F. Place beans in 11×7-inch glass baking dish. Combine beer, onion, ketchup, molasses, Worcestershire sauce, mustard and ginger in medium bowl. Pour over beans; toss to coat.

2 Cut bacon into 1-inch pieces; arrange in single layer over beans. Bake, uncovered, 40 to 45 minutes or until most liquid is absorbed and bacon is browned.

Southern Macaroni and Cheese

MAKES 4 SERVINGS

2 teaspoons all-purpose flour

1 tablespoon dry mustard

Salt and black pepper

1 cup milk

½ cup plus 1 tablespoon shredded sharp Cheddar cheese, divided

1 egg white

1½ cups cooked whole wheat or multigrain elbow macaroni

1 tablespoon panko or plain dry bread crumbs

⅛ teaspoon paprika

1 Preheat oven to 325°F. Spray 1-quart baking dish with nonstick cooking spray.

2 Combine flour, mustard, salt and pepper in small saucepan; whisk in milk. Cook and stir over medium heat until mixture is bubbly and thickened. Remove from heat; let stand 2 to 3 minutes. Stir in ½ cup cheese until melted.

3 Stir egg white into macaroni in large bowl. Stir in cheese sauce. Spoon into prepared dish. Combine remaining 1 tablespoon cheese, panko and paprika; mix well. Sprinkle over macaroni.

4 Bake 15 to 20 minutes or until bubbly and lightly browned. Let stand 5 minutes before serving.

Boston Brown Bread Muffins ▶

MAKES 12 MUFFINS

★ ★

½ cup rye flour
½ cup whole wheat flour
½ cup yellow cornmeal
1½ teaspoons baking soda
¾ teaspoon salt
1 cup buttermilk
⅓ cup packed dark brown sugar
⅓ cup molasses
⅓ cup dark beer
1 egg
1 cup golden raisins
    Cream cheese, softened

1 Preheat oven to 400°F. Grease 12 standard (2½-inch) muffin cups or line with paper baking cups.

2 Combine flours, cornmeal, baking soda and salt in large bowl. Combine buttermilk, brown sugar, molasses, beer and egg in medium bowl. Add to flour mixture along with raisins; stir until combined. Spoon batter into prepared muffin cups, filling three-fourths full.

3 Bake 15 minutes or until toothpick inserted into centers comes out clean. Serve with cream cheese.

Southern Pecan Cornbread Stuffing

MAKES 8 SERVINGS

★ ★

5 cups dry cornbread stuffing mix
1 package KNORR® Leek Recipe Mix
½ cup (1 stick) I CAN'T BELIEVE IT'S NOT BUTTER!® Spread
1 cup coarsely chopped pecans
1 package (10 ounces) frozen corn, thawed and drained
1 cup hot water
1 cup orange juice

1 Preheat oven to 350°F. In large bowl, combine stuffing and recipe mix.

2 In 8-inch skillet, melt I Can't Believe It's Not Butter!® Spread over medium heat and cook pecans, stirring occasionally, 5 minutes.

3 Add corn, water, orange juice and pecan mixture to stuffing; toss until moistened. Spoon into 2-quart casserole sprayed with cooking spray.

4 Cover and bake 30 minutes or until heated through.

Cajun Dirty Rice ▶

MAKES 6 SERVINGS

½ pound pork sausage, crumbled

1 small onion, finely chopped

1 stalk celery, finely chopped

1 small clove garlic, minced

2 cups chicken broth

1 tablespoon Cajun seasoning

2 cups MINUTE® White Rice, uncooked

Cook sausage in medium skillet over medium heat until evenly browned, stirring occasionally.

Add onions, celery and garlic; cook and stir 5 minutes or until sausage is cooked through and vegetables are tender.

Add broth to skillet with seasoning; stir. Bring to a boil. Stir in rice; cover. Remove from heat. Let stand 5 minutes. Fluff with fork.

VARIATION

For a more authentic dish, reduce sausage to ¼ pound and add ¼ pound chopped chicken livers.

Broccoli with Cheese Sauce

MAKES 3 TO 4 SERVINGS

12 ounces fresh broccoli, cut into spears with 2- or 3-inch stems

8 ounces pasteurized process cheese product, cubed

3 tablespoons milk

½ teaspoon Worcestershire sauce

MICROWAVE DIRECTIONS

1 Arrange broccoli spears on microwavable dinner plate with stalks toward outside of plate; cover with vented plastic wrap. Microwave on HIGH 3 to 4 minutes or until broccoli stems are tender.

2 Combine cheese product, milk and Worcestershire sauce in 2-quart glass measuring cup. Microwave on HIGH 2 minutes; stir. If cheese product is not completely melted, microwave 1 minute more, stirring after 30 seconds, until melted. Serve sauce over broccoli.

Loaded Baked Potatoes

MAKES 4 SERVINGS

4 large baking potatoes

1 cup (4 ounces) shredded Cheddar cheese

1 cup (4 ounces) shredded Monterey Jack cheese

8 slices bacon, crisp-cooked

½ cup sour cream

¼ cup (½ stick) butter, melted

2 tablespoons milk

1 teaspoon salt

¼ teaspoon black pepper

1 tablespoon vegetable oil

2 teaspoons coarse salt

1 green onion, thinly sliced (optional)

1 Preheat oven to 400°F. Prick potatoes all over with fork; place in small baking pan. Bake 1 hour or until potatoes are fork-tender. Let stand until cool enough to handle. *Reduce oven temperature to 350°F.*

2 Combine Cheddar and Monterey Jack cheeses in small bowl; reserve ¼ cup for garnish. Chop bacon; reserve ¼ cup for garnish.

3 Cut off thin slice from one long side of each potato. Scoop out centers of potatoes, leaving ¼-inch shell. Place flesh from 3 potatoes in medium bowl. (Reserve flesh from fourth potato for another use.) Add sour cream, butter, remaining 1¾ cups shredded cheese, bacon, milk, 1 teaspoon salt and pepper to bowl with potatoes; mash until well blended.

4 Turn potato shells over; brush bottoms and sides with oil. Sprinkle evenly with coarse salt. Turn right side up and return to baking pan. Fill shells with mashed potato mixture, mounding over tops of shells. Sprinkle with reserved cheese and bacon.

5 Bake 20 minutes or until filling is hot and cheese is melted. Garnish with green onion.

Home-Style Macaroni and Cheese

MAKES 4 SERVINGS

10 ounces uncooked elbow macaroni

7½ teaspoons plain dry bread crumbs

¼ teaspoon dried parsley flakes

¼ teaspoon dried oregano

2 tablespoons chopped fresh parsley

1 tablespoon grated Parmesan cheese

6 ounces pasteurized process cheese spread, cut into ½-inch cubes

1 cup milk

2 egg whites

Salt and black pepper

3 plum tomatoes, cut crosswise into ⅛-inch rounds

1 Preheat oven to 325°F.

2 Spray 9-inch square baking pan with nonstick cooking spray; set aside. Cook pasta according to package directions, omitting salt; drain. Place pasta in bottom of prepared pan.

3 Combine bread crumbs, dried parsley flakes, oregano, fresh parsley and Parmesan cheese in small bowl; set aside.

4 Combine cheese spread and milk in medium saucepan. Cook over medium heat until melted, stirring constantly. Remove from heat; whisk in egg whites until completely blended. Pour over pasta; sprinkle with salt and pepper.

5 Arrange tomato slices on top of pasta; sprinkle evenly with bread crumb mixture. Lightly spray top of bread crumbs with cooking spray. Bake 35 minutes or until heated through. Let stand 5 minutes before serving.

NOTE

For a spicier dish use pasteurized process cheese spread with mild jalapeño peppers.

Green Bean Casserole with Homemade French Fried Onions

MAKES 6 TO 8 SERVINGS

6 cups water

1 pound fresh green beans, cut into 2-inch pieces

1 tablespoon vegetable oil

8 ounces cremini mushrooms, chopped

3 tablespoons butter

3 tablespoons rice flour

1 teaspoon salt

¼ teaspoon red pepper flakes

1 cup vegetable broth

1 cup whole milk

Homemade French Fried Onions (recipe follows)

1 Preheat oven to 350°F. Spray 13×9-inch baking dish with nonstick cooking spray.

2 Bring water to a boil in medium saucepan. Add green beans; cook 4 minutes. Drain.

3 Heat oil in large saucepan over medium heat. Add mushrooms; cook and stir 8 minutes. Add butter; cook and stir until melted. Stir in rice flour, salt and red pepper flakes. Gradually stir in broth and milk; cook and stir until thickened. Remove from heat; stir in green beans. Pour into prepared dish.

4 Bake 30 minutes. Meanwhile, prepare Homemade French Fried Onions.

5 Remove casserole from oven. Top with Homemade French Fried Onions; bake 5 minutes.

Homemade French Fried Onions

MAKES ABOUT 1½ CUPS

2 small onions, sliced into rings

½ cup whole milk

½ cup rice flour

½ cup cornmeal

1 teaspoon salt

½ teaspoon black pepper

Vegetable oil

1 Line baking sheet with paper towels. Separate onion rings and spread in shallow dish. Pour milk over onions; toss to coat. Combine rice flour, cornmeal, salt and pepper in large resealable food storage bag; mix well.

2 Heat oil in large heavy skillet over medium-high heat until temperature registers 300° to 325°F on deep-fry thermometer.

3 Working in batches, add onion rings to large resealable food storage bag; shake to coat. Add onions to oil; fry 2 minutes per side or until golden brown. Remove to prepared baking sheet using slotted spoon. Repeat with remaining onions.

Country Time Macaroni Salad

MAKES 6 SERVINGS

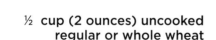

½ cup (2 ounces) uncooked regular or whole wheat elbow macaroni

3 tablespoons mayonnaise

2 tablespoons plain yogurt

2 teaspoons sweet pickle relish

¾ teaspoon dried dill weed

½ teaspoon prepared yellow mustard (optional)

¼ teaspoon salt

½ cup thawed frozen green peas

½ cup chopped green bell pepper

⅓ cup thinly sliced celery

4 ounces ham, cubed

4 tablespoons (1 ounce) shredded Cheddar cheese, divided

1 Cook pasta according to package directions, omitting salt and fat; drain and rinse under cold running water until completely cooled.

2 Meanwhile, combine mayonnaise, yogurt, relish, dill weed, mustard, if desired, and salt in small bowl; stir until well blended.

3 Combine peas, bell pepper, celery and ham in medium bowl.

4 Add pasta and mayonnaise mixture to pea mixture; mix well. Stir in 2 tablespoons cheese; toss lightly. Sprinkle with remaining 2 tablespoons cheese. Serve immediately.

Crispy Smashed Potatoes ▶

MAKES ABOUT 6 SERVINGS

1 tablespoon plus
   ½ teaspoon salt, divided

3 pounds unpeeled small
   red potatoes (2 inches
   or smaller)

4 tablespoons (½ stick)
   butter, melted, divided

¼ teaspoon black pepper

½ cup grated Parmesan
   cheese (optional)

1 Fill large saucepan three-fourths full of water; add 1 tablespoon salt. Bring to a boil over high heat. Add potatoes; boil 20 minutes or until potatoes are tender when pierced with tip of sharp knife. Drain potatoes; set aside until cool enough to handle.

2 Preheat oven to 450°F. Brush large baking sheet with 2 tablespoons butter. Working with one potato at a time, smash with hand or bottom of measuring cup to about ½-inch thickness. Arrange smashed potatoes in single layer on prepared baking sheet. Brush with remaining 2 tablespoons butter; sprinkle with remaining ½ teaspoon salt and pepper.

3 Bake 30 to 40 minutes or until bottoms of potatoes are golden brown. Turn potatoes. Bake 10 minutes. Sprinkle with cheese, if desired. Bake 5 minutes or until cheese is melted.

Sweet Potato Fries

MAKES 2 SERVINGS

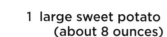

1 large sweet potato
   (about 8 ounces)

2 teaspoons olive oil

¼ teaspoon coarse salt

¼ teaspoon black pepper

¼ teaspoon ground red
   pepper

   Honey or maple syrup
   (optional)

1 Preheat oven to 425°F. Lightly spray baking sheet with nonstick cooking spray.

2 Peel sweet potato; cut lengthwise into long spears. Toss with oil, salt, black pepper and red pepper on prepared baking sheet. Arrange sweet potato spears in single layer not touching.

3 Bake 20 to 30 minutes or until lightly browned, turning halfway through baking time. Serve with honey, if desired.

Crunchy Asparagus ▶

MAKES 4 SERVINGS

★ ★

1 package (10 ounces) frozen asparagus cuts

1 teaspoon lemon juice

3 to 4 drops hot pepper sauce

¼ teaspoon salt

¼ teaspoon dried basil

⅛ teaspoon black pepper

2 teaspoons sunflower kernels

Lemon slices (optional)

MICROWAVE DIRECTIONS

1 Place asparagus and 2 tablespoons water in 1-quart microwavable casserole dish; cover. Microwave on HIGH 4½ to 5½ minutes or until asparagus is hot, stirring halfway through cooking time to break apart. Drain. Cover; set aside.

2 Combine lemon juice, hot pepper sauce, salt, basil and pepper in small bowl; stir to blend. Pour mixture over asparagus; toss to coat. Sprinkle with sunflower kernels. Garnish with lemon slices, if desired.

Roasted Garlic Mashed Potatoes

MAKES 6 TO 8 SERVINGS

★ ★

REYNOLDS WRAP®
Aluminum Foil

2 large bulbs garlic

1 teaspoon olive oil

3 pounds large red potatoes, peeled and cubed

¼ cup milk, heated

¼ cup (½ stick) butter, softened

Salt and black pepper

1 tablespoon chopped fresh parsley

PREHEAT oven to 400°F. Slice top of bulbs off unpeeled garlic. Remove papery outer layer of garlic bulbs. Place garlic on a sheet of REYNOLDS WRAP® Aluminum Foil. Drizzle with olive oil. Wrap in foil; place on a cookie sheet.

BAKE 25 minutes or until garlic is soft. Cool. Squeeze pulp from garlic and mash in a bowl; set aside.

PLACE potatoes in large saucepan. Cook, covered, in boiling lightly salted water 20 to 25 minutes or until tender. Drain. Mash with potato masher or beat with electric mixer on low speed. Add roasted garlic, milk, butter, salt and pepper to taste. Beat until light and fluffy. Stir in parsley.

Slow-Cooked Succotash ▶

MAKES 8 SERVINGS

2 teaspoons canola oil

1 cup diced onion

1 cup diced green bell pepper

1 cup diced celery

1 teaspoon paprika

1½ cups frozen yellow or white corn

1½ cups frozen lima beans

1 cup canned diced tomatoes

2 teaspoons dried parsley flakes *or* 1 tablespoon minced fresh parsley

½ teaspoon salt

½ teaspoon black pepper

SLOW COOKER DIRECTIONS

1 Heat oil in large skillet over medium heat. Add onion, bell pepper and celery; cook and stir 5 minutes or until onion is translucent and bell pepper and celery are crisp-tender.

2 Combine onion mixture, paprika, corn, beans, tomatoes, parsley flakes, salt and black pepper in slow cooker; stir to blend. Cover; cook on LOW 6 to 8 hours or on HIGH 3 to 4 hours.

Super-Moist Cornbread

MAKES 8 SERVINGS

1 can (11 ounces) Mexican-style corn, drained

1 package (8½ ounces) corn muffin mix

½ cup HELLMANN'S® or BEST FOODS® Real Mayonnaise

1 egg, slightly beaten

1 Preheat oven to 400°F. Spray 8-inch round cake pan with nonstick cooking spray; set aside.

2 In medium bowl, combine all ingredients until moistened. Evenly spread in prepared pan.

3 Bake 25 minutes or until toothpick inserted into center comes out clean.

Crispy Oven Fries
with Herbed Dipping Sauce

MAKES 3 SERVINGS

★ ★ ★ ★ ★ ★ ★ ★ ★ ★ ★ ★ ★ ★ ★ ★ ★ ★ ★

Herbed Dipping Sauce
(recipe follows)
2 large unpeeled baking
   potatoes
2 tablespoons vegetable oil
1 teaspoon kosher salt

1 Preheat oven to 425°F. Line two baking sheets with foil; spray with nonstick cooking spray. Prepare Herbed Dipping Sauce; set aside.

2 Cut potatoes lengthwise into ¼-inch slices, then cut each slice into ¼-inch strips. Combine potato strips and oil on prepared baking sheets. Toss to coat evenly; arrange in single layer.

3 Bake 25 minutes. Turn fries over; bake 15 minutes or until light golden brown and crisp. Sprinkle with salt. Serve immediately with Herbed Dipping Sauce.

★ ★ ★ ★ ★ ★

HERBED DIPPING SAUCE

Stir ½ cup mayonnaise, 2 tablespoons chopped fresh herbs (such as basil, parsley, oregano and/or dill), 1 teaspoon salt and ½ teaspoon black pepper in small bowl until smooth and well blended. Cover; refrigerate until ready to serve.

SPARKLING DESSERTS

All-American Chocolate Chip Cookies

MAKES ABOUT 1½ DOZEN COOKIES

2½ cups all-purpose flour

1 teaspoon baking soda

½ teaspoon salt

1 cup (2 sticks) butter, softened

1 cup packed light brown sugar

½ cup granulated sugar

2 eggs

1 tablespoon vanilla

1 package (12 ounces) semisweet chocolate chips

1 cup coarsely chopped walnuts (optional)

1 Preheat oven to 350°F. Combine flour, baking soda and salt in medium bowl.

2 Beat butter, brown sugar and granulated sugar in large bowl with electric mixer at medium speed until light and fluffy. Beat in eggs and vanilla. Add flour mixture to butter mixture; beat until well blended. Stir in chocolate chips and walnuts, if desired.

3 Drop dough by ¼ cupfuls about 3 inches apart onto ungreased cookie sheets. Bake 12 to 14 minutes or until edges are light golden brown. Cool 2 minutes on cookie sheets. Remove cookies to wire racks; cool completely.

VARIATION

For smaller cookies, preheat oven to 375°F. Prepare dough as directed; drop heaping teaspoonfuls onto ungreased cookie sheets. Bake 8 to 10 minutes or until edges are golden brown. Makes about 6 dozen cookies.

161

Steamed Southern Sweet Potato Custard

MAKES 4 SERVINGS

1 can (16 ounces) cut sweet potatoes, drained

1 can (12 ounces) evaporated milk, divided

½ cup packed light brown sugar

2 eggs, lightly beaten

1 teaspoon ground cinnamon

½ teaspoon ground ginger

¼ teaspoon salt

Whipped cream (optional)

Ground nutmeg (optional)

SLOW COOKER DIRECTIONS

1 Process sweet potatoes and ¼ cup evaporated milk in food processor or blender until smooth. Add remaining milk, brown sugar, eggs, cinnamon, ginger and salt; process until well blended. Pour into ungreased 1-quart soufflé dish. Cover tightly with foil. Crumple large sheet of foil (about 15×12 inches); place in bottom of slow cooker. Pour 2 cups water over foil. Make foil handles.*

2 Transfer dish to slow cooker using foil handles. Cover; cook on HIGH 2½ to 3 hours or until skewer inserted into center comes out clean.

3 Use foil handles to lift dish from slow cooker; transfer to wire rack. Uncover; let stand 30 minutes. Garnish with whipped cream and nutmeg.

To make foil handles, tear off three 18×3-inch strips of heavy-duty foil. Crisscross the strips so they resemble the spokes of a wheel. Place the dish in the center of the strips. Pull the foil strips up and over the dish and place it into the slow cooker. Leave the foil strips in while the food cooks, so you can easily lift the item out again when it is finished cooking.

All-American Cookie Pie

MAKES 8 SERVINGS

1 refrigerated pie crust (half of 15-ounce package)

¾ cup (1½ sticks) butter, softened

½ cup granulated sugar

½ cup packed brown sugar

½ teaspoon vanilla

2 eggs

¾ cup all-purpose flour

1 cup (6 ounces) semisweet chocolate chunks or chips

1 cup chopped nuts

1 Preheat oven to 325°F. Line 9-inch pie plate with crust; flute edge as desired.

2 Beat butter, granulated sugar, brown sugar and vanilla in large bowl with electric mixer at medium speed until light and fluffy. Add eggs; beat until well blended. Beat in flour just until blended. Stir in chocolate chunks and nuts. Spread evenly in crust.

3 Bake 65 to 70 minutes or until toothpick inserted into center comes out clean. Cool completely on wire rack.

Boston Cream Pie

MAKES 16 SERVINGS

1 package (about 15 ounces) yellow cake plus ingredients to prepare mix

Cream Filling (recipe follows)

Chocolate Glaze (recipe follows)

1 Preheat oven to 350°F. Spray two 9-inch round cake pans with nonstick cooking spray.

2 Prepare and bake cake in prepared pans according to package directions. Cool cake layers in pans 10 minutes. Loosen edges; invert onto wire racks to cool completely.

3 Meanwhile, prepare Cream Filling. When filling is cool, prepare Chocolate Glaze. To assemble, place one cake layer on plate. Spread Cream Filling over cake layer; top with second layer. Spread with Chocolate Glaze; let stand until glaze is set.

CREAM FILLING

Combine ⅓ cup granulated sugar, 2 tablespoons cornstarch and ¼ teaspoon salt in medium saucepan. Gradually stir in 1½ cups milk; cook over medium heat until mixture thickens and comes to a boil, stirring constantly. Boil 1 minute, stirring constantly. Stir small amount of hot milk mixture into 2 beaten egg yolks until well blended. Pour egg yolk mixture back into milk mixture in saucepan. Bring to a boil; boil 1 minute, stirring constantly. *Do not overcook.* Remove from heat; stir in 2 teaspoons vanilla. Cool to room temperature.

CHOCOLATE GLAZE

Combine 2 ounces unsweetened chocolate and 3 tablespoons butter in medium saucepan; stir over low heat until melted. Remove from heat; stir in 1 cup sifted powdered sugar and 1 teaspoon vanilla until well blended. Stir in 3 to 5 teaspoons water, 1 teaspoon at a time, until glaze reaches desired consistency. Cool slightly.

Flag Cookies

MAKES ABOUT 1½ DOZEN COOKIES

★ ★ ★ ★ ★ ★ ★ ★ ★ ★ ★ ★ ★ ★ ★ ★ ★ ★ ★ ★

1 package (18 ounces) refrigerated sugar cookie dough

Red food coloring

1 aerosol can (6.4 ounces) blue decorating icing, with star tip attached

White sprinkles

1. Remove dough from wrapper; divide in half. Wrap 1 half in plastic wrap; refrigerate. Place remaining half in medium bowl; let stand at room temperature about 15 minutes.

2. Add red food coloring to dough in bowl; beat at medium speed of electric mixer until evenly colored. Wrap dough in plastic wrap; refrigerate 20 minutes.

3. Roll red dough on lightly floured surface to form 9-inch square. Repeat with plain dough; place plain dough on top of red dough. Cut square into three (3-inch) strips. Stack strips, alternating colors, to create one rectangular log about 9 inches long and 3 inches wide. Place on flat plate and wrap in plastic wrap; freeze 15 minutes or until firm.

4. Preheat oven to 350°F. Grease cookie sheets. Cut dough into ⅓-inch slices; place on prepared cookie sheets.

5. Bake 8 to 10 minutes or until cookies are lightly browned at edges. Cool on cookie sheets 3 minutes; remove to wire racks to cool completely.

6. Pipe 1-inch square of blue icing onto upper left corners of cookies; top with sprinkles.

Key Lime Pie

MAKES 8 SERVINGS

12 whole graham crackers*

⅓ cup butter, melted

3 tablespoons sugar

2 cans (14 ounces each) sweetened condensed milk

¾ cup key lime juice

6 egg yolks

Pinch salt

Whipped cream (optional)

Lime slices (optional)

Or substitute 1½ cups graham cracker crumbs.

1 Preheat oven to 350°F. Spray 9-inch pie plate or springform pan with nonstick cooking spray.

2 Place graham crackers in food processor; pulse until coarse crumbs form. Add butter and sugar; pulse until well blended. Press mixture onto bottom and 1 inch up side of prepared pie plate. Bake 8 minutes or until lightly browned. Remove to wire rack to cool 10 minutes. *Reduce oven temperature to 325°F.*

3 Meanwhile, beat sweetened condensed milk, lime juice, egg yolks and salt in large bowl with electric mixer at medium-low speed 1 minute or until well blended and smooth. Pour into crust.

4 Bake 20 minutes or until set. Cool completely on wire rack. Cover; refrigerate 2 hours or overnight. Garnish with whipped cream and lime slices.

Independence Day Flag Cake

MAKES 12 TO 15 SERVINGS

¾ cup (1½ sticks) butter or margarine, softened

1⅔ cups sugar

3 eggs

1 teaspoon vanilla extract

2 cups all-purpose flour

⅔ cup HERSHEY'®S Cocoa

1¼ teaspoons baking soda

1 teaspoon salt

¼ teaspoon baking powder

1⅓ cups water

Vanilla Buttercream Frosting (recipe follows)

½ pint blueberries

1 quart small strawberries, of uniform size

1 Heat oven to 350°F. Grease and flour 13×9×2-inch baking pan.

2 Combine butter, sugar, eggs and vanilla in large bowl; beat on high speed of mixer 3 minutes. Stir together flour, cocoa, baking soda, salt and baking powder; add alternately with water to butter mixture, beating on low speed after each addition just until blended. Pour into prepared pan.

3 Bake 30 to 35 minutes or until wooden pick inserted in center comes out clean. Cool 10 minutes; remove from pan to wire rack. Cool completely.

4 Place cake on oblong serving tray or foil-covered cardboard. Prepare Vanilla Buttercream Frosting; spread over top and sides of cake. Arrange blueberries in upper left corner of cake, creating a 5×4-inch rectangle. Arrange strawberries in rows for red stripes.

Vanilla Buttercream Frosting

MAKES ABOUT 3 CUPS

3 cups powdered sugar

⅓ cup butter or margarine, softened

2 tablespoons milk

1½ teaspoons vanilla extract

Combine powdered sugar and butter in large bowl. Add milk and vanilla; beat until smooth and of spreading consistency. Add additional milk, 1 teaspoon at a time, if needed.

Snickery Pie

MAKES 8 TO 10 SERVINGS

CRUST

- 1½ cups vanilla wafer cookie crumbs
- 3 tablespoons sugar
- 2 tablespoons unsweetened cocoa powder
- ¼ cup (½ stick) butter, melted

FILLING

- 2 cups whipping cream
- 1 package (8 ounces) cream cheese, softened
- ¾ cup dulce de leche
- ¼ cup sugar
- 1 teaspoon vanilla
- 2 chocolate-covered peanut-nougat-caramel candy bars (1.86 ounces each), finely chopped

TOPPING

- ¼ cup dulce de leche
- 3 tablespoons milk
- ½ cup semisweet chocolate chips
- 1½ teaspoons coconut oil
- 2 chocolate-covered peanut-nougat-caramel candy bars (1.86 ounces each), coarsely chopped
- ¼ cup coarsely chopped salted peanuts

1 For crust, preheat oven to 350°F. Combine cookie crumbs, 3 tablespoons sugar and cocoa in medium bowl; mix well. Stir in butter until moistened and well blended. Press mixture onto bottom and up side of 9-inch deep-dish pie plate. Bake 8 minutes. Cool completely on wire rack.

2 For filling, beat 2 cups cream in large bowl with electric mixer at medium-high speed 1 minute or until stiff peaks form. Transfer cream to medium bowl. (Do not wash out mixer bowl.)

3 Combine cream cheese, ¾ cup dulce de leche, ¼ cup sugar and vanilla in same large bowl. Beat at medium speed 1 to 2 minutes or until well blended, scraping bowl once.

4 Gently fold in whipped cream in three additions until well blended (no streaks of white remain). Fold in 2 chopped candy bars. Spread evenly in prepared crust. Refrigerate 4 hours or overnight.

5 For topping, microwave ¼ cup dulce de leche in small bowl on HIGH 20 seconds. Stir. Microwave 10 seconds or until softened. Stir in milk until well blended. Combine chocolate and coconut oil in small saucepan; heat over low heat until chocolate is melted and mixture is smooth, stirring frequently. Sprinkle 2 chopped candy bars and peanuts over top of pie; drizzle with dulce de leche and chocolate mixtures. Refrigerate until topping is set.

Ultimate Banana Bread

MAKES 6 SERVINGS

1¾ cups all-purpose flour
1 teaspoon baking soda
½ teaspoon salt
½ teaspoon ground cinnamon
¼ teaspoon ground nutmeg
2 eggs
3 very ripe bananas, mashed (about 1½ cups)
1 cup packed brown sugar
½ cup vegetable oil
½ cup sour cream
1 teaspoon vanilla
1 cup coarsely chopped walnuts, toasted

SAUCE AND GARNISH
¼ cup (½ stick) butter
½ cup packed brown sugar
½ cup whipping cream
Pinch salt
2 teaspoons brandy
2 ripe bananas, sliced
¼ cup sliced almonds
Vanilla ice cream or whipped cream

1 Preheat oven to 350°F. Spray 9×5-inch loaf pan with nonstick cooking spray.

2 Combine flour, baking soda, ½ teaspoon salt, cinnamon and nutmeg in large bowl; mix well. Beat eggs in medium bowl. Add mashed bananas, 1 cup brown sugar, oil, sour cream and vanilla; stir until well blended. Add to flour mixture; stir just until blended. Fold in walnuts. Spread batter in prepared pan.

3 Bake 50 to 55 minutes or until toothpick inserted into center comes out clean. Cool in pan 10 minutes; remove to wire rack to cool while preparing sauce.

4 For sauce, melt butter in small saucepan over medium heat. Add ½ cup brown sugar; stir until dissolved. Add cream and pinch of salt; bring to a boil, stirring constantly. Remove from heat; stir in brandy.

5 Cut loaf into 12 slices; place two slices on each of six serving plates. Pour sauce over banana bread; top with sliced bananas, almonds and ice cream. Drizzle with additional sauce.

Chocolate Cake Milkshake

MAKES 1 SERVING

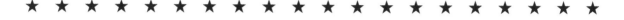

1 slice (⅛ of cake) Rich Chocolate Cake (recipe follows)

½ cup milk

2 scoops vanilla ice cream (about 1 cup total)

1 Prepare and frost Rich Chocolate Cake.

2 Combine milk, ice cream and cake slice in blender; blend just until cake is incorporated but texture of shake is not completely smooth.

Rich Chocolate Cake

MAKES 8 TO 10 SERVINGS

1 package (about 15 ounces) devil's food cake mix

1 cup cold water

1 cup mayonnaise

3 eggs

1½ containers (16 ounces each) chocolate frosting

1 Preheat oven to 350°F. Spray two 9-inch round cake pans with nonstick cooking spray.

2 Beat cake mix, water, mayonnaise and eggs in large bowl with electric mixer at low speed 30 seconds. Beat at medium speed 2 minutes. Pour batter into prepared pans.

3 Bake 25 minutes or until toothpick inserted into centers comes out clean. Cool in pans 10 minutes; remove to wire racks to cool completely.

4 Fill and frost cake with chocolate frosting.

Crunchy Ice Cream Pie ▶

MAKES 6 SERVINGS

8 ounces semisweet chocolate, chopped

2 tablespoons butter

1½ cups crisp rice cereal

½ gallon chocolate chip or fudge ripple ice cream, softened

Hot fudge dessert topping

1 Spray 9-inch pie plate with nonstick cooking spray.

2 Combine chocolate and butter in top of double boiler over simmering water; stir until chocolate is melted and mixture is smooth. Remove from heat. Add cereal; stir until well blended.

3 Spoon mixture into prepared pie plate; press onto bottom and 1 inch up side to form crust. Spread ice cream evenly in crust. Cover and freeze until ready to serve.

4 Let pie stand at room temperature 10 minutes before serving. Drizzle with hot fudge topping.

Shortcut Pecan Pie

MAKES 8 SERVINGS

½ (16-ounce) package refrigerated sugar cookie dough

¼ cup all-purpose flour

3 eggs

¾ cup dark corn syrup

¾ cup sugar

1 teaspoon vanilla

¼ teaspoon salt

2 cups chopped pecans

1 Preheat oven to 350°F. Lightly spray 9-inch pie plate with nonstick cooking spray. Let dough stand at room temperature 15 minutes.

2 Beat dough and flour in large bowl with electric mixer at medium speed until well blended. Press dough evenly into bottom and ½ inch up side of prepared pie plate. Crimp edge with fork. Bake 20 minutes.

3 Meanwhile, beat eggs in large bowl. Add corn syrup, sugar, vanilla and salt; beat until well blended. Pour into crust; sprinkle evenly with pecans.

4 Bake 40 to 45 minutes or just until center is set. Cool completely on wire rack.

Best-Ever Apple Pie

MAKES ONE (9-INCH) PIE

- 2⅓ cups all-purpose flour, divided
- ¾ cup plus 1 tablespoon sugar, divided
- ½ teaspoon baking powder
- ½ teaspoon salt
- ¾ cup plus 3 tablespoons cold unsalted butter, cut into small pieces, divided
- 4 to 5 tablespoons ice water
- 1 egg, separated
- 7 medium Jonathan or Granny Smith apples, peeled, cored and sliced
- 1 tablespoon lemon juice
- 1¼ teaspoons ground cinnamon
- 1 tablespoon sour cream

1 Combine 2 cups flour, 1 tablespoon sugar, baking powder and salt in large bowl until well blended. Cut in ¾ cup butter using pastry blender or two knives until mixture resembles coarse crumbs. Add water, 1 tablespoon at a time, to flour mixture. Toss with fork until mixture holds together. Form dough into two discs. Wrap discs in plastic wrap; refrigerate 30 minutes or until firm.

2 Working with one disc at a time, roll out dough on lightly floured surface with lightly floured rolling pin into 12-inch circle, ⅛ inch thick. Ease dough into 9-inch glass pie plate. *Do not stretch dough.* Trim dough leaving ½-inch overhang; brush with egg white. Set aside.

3 Preheat oven to 450°F.

4 Place apple slices in large bowl; sprinkle with lemon juice. Combine remaining ⅓ cup flour, ¾ cup sugar and cinnamon in small bowl until well blended. Add to apple mixture; toss to coat apples evenly. Spoon filling into prepared pie crust; place remaining 3 tablespoons butter on top of filling.

5 Roll out remaining dough disc into 10-inch circle. Cut into ½-inch-wide strips. Arrange in lattice design over apples. Seal and flute edge. Combine egg yolk and sour cream in small bowl until well blended. Cover; refrigerate until ready to use.

6 Bake pie 10 minutes. *Reduce oven temperature to 375°F.* Bake 35 minutes. Brush egg yolk mixture evenly on pie crust with pastry brush. Bake 20 to 25 minutes or until crust is deep golden brown. Cool completely on wire rack. Store loosely covered at room temperature 1 day, or refrigerate up to 4 days.

Basic Oatmeal Cookies

MAKES 3 DOZEN COOKIES

2 cups old-fashioned oats

1⅓ cups all-purpose flour

¾ teaspoon baking soda

½ teaspoon baking powder

½ teaspoon salt

1 cup packed brown sugar

¾ cup (1½ sticks) butter, softened

¼ cup granulated sugar

1 egg

1 tablespoon honey

1 teaspoon vanilla

1 Preheat oven to 350°F. Line cookie sheets with parchment paper.

2 Combine oats, flour, baking soda, baking powder and salt in medium bowl.

3 Beat brown sugar, butter and granulated sugar in large bowl with electric mixer at medium speed until light and fluffy. Add egg, honey and vanilla; beat until well blended. Gradually add flour mixture about ½ cup at a time; beat at low speed just until blended. Drop dough by tablespoonfuls about 2 inches apart onto prepared cookie sheets.

4 Bake 11 to 15 minutes or until cookies are puffed and golden. *Do not overbake.* Cool 5 minutes on cookie sheets. Remove to wire racks; cool completely.

All-American Cupcakes

MAKES 22 CUPCAKES

1 package (about 18 ounces) cake mix, any flavor, plus ingredients to prepare mix

1 container (16 ounces) white frosting

Blue candy stars

Red string licorice

1 Preheat oven to 350°F. Line 22 standard (2½-inch) muffin cups with paper baking cups. Prepare cake mix according to package directions. Spoon batter into prepared muffin cups, filling two-thirds full.

2 Bake 20 minutes or until toothpick inserted into centers comes out clean. Cool in pans 10 minutes. Remove to wire racks; cool completely.

3 Frost cupcakes. Arrange candy stars in left corner of each cupcake. Arrange licorice in rows across remaining portion of each cupcake, cutting pieces to fit.

★ ★ ★ ★ ★ ★

TIP

Blue candy stars can be found in the bulk section of candy stores and at some craft stores. If you can't find them, you can substitute mini candy-coated chocolate pieces or blue candy dots.

INDEX

★ ★ ★ ★ ★ ★

ACKNOWLEDGMENTS

**The publisher would like to thank the companies listed below
for the use of their recipes and photographs in this publication.**

Campbell Soup Company
Dole Food Company, Inc.
The Hershey Company
McCormick®
Recipes courtesy of the Reynolds Kitchens
Riviana Foods Inc.
© 2021 Sunbeam Products, Inc. doing business
as Jarden Consumer Solutions.

Unilever

VOLUME MEASUREMENTS (dry)

1/8 teaspoon = 0.5 mL
1/4 teaspoon = 1 mL
1/2 teaspoon = 2 mL
3/4 teaspoon = 4 mL
1 teaspoon = 5 mL
1 tablespoon = 15 mL
2 tablespoons = 30 mL
1/4 cup = 60 mL
1/3 cup = 75 mL
1/2 cup = 125 mL
2/3 cup = 150 mL
3/4 cup = 175 mL
1 cup = 250 mL
2 cups = 1 pint = 500 mL
3 cups = 750 mL
4 cups = 1 quart = 1 L

VOLUME MEASUREMENTS (fluid)

1 fluid ounce (2 tablespoons) = 30 mL
4 fluid ounces (1/2 cup) = 125 mL
8 fluid ounces (1 cup) = 250 mL
12 fluid ounces (1 1/2 cups) = 375 mL
16 fluid ounces (2 cups) = 500 mL

WEIGHTS (mass)

1/2 ounce = 15 g
1 ounce = 30 g
3 ounces = 90 g
4 ounces = 120 g
8 ounces = 225 g
10 ounces = 285 g
12 ounces = 360 g
16 ounces = 1 pound = 450 g

DIMENSIONS

1/16 inch = 2 mm
1/8 inch = 3 mm
1/4 inch = 6 mm
1/2 inch = 1.5 cm
3/4 inch = 2 cm
1 inch = 2.5 cm

OVEN TEMPERATURES

250°F = 120°C
275°F = 140°C
300°F = 150°C
325°F = 160°C
350°F = 180°C
375°F = 190°C
400°F = 200°C
425°F = 220°C
450°F = 230°C

BAKING PAN SIZES

Utensil	Size in Inches/Quarts	Metric Volume	Size in Centimeters
Baking or Cake Pan (square or rectangular)	8×8×2	2 L	20×20×5
	9×9×2	2.5 L	23×23×5
	12×8×2	3 L	30×20×5
	13×9×2	3.5 L	33×23×5
Loaf Pan	8×4×3	1.5 L	20×10×7
	9×5×3	2 L	23×13×7
Round Layer Cake Pan	8×1½	1.2 L	20×4
	9×1½	1.5 L	23×4
Pie Plate	8×1¼	750 mL	20×3
	9×1¼	1 L	23×3
Baking Dish or Casserole	1 quart	1 L	—
	1½ quart	1.5 L	—
	2 quart	2 L	—